Being *a* Believer *in* *an* Unbelieving World

Contemporary Reflections on the Sermon on the Mount

WAYNE BROUWER

Being a Believer in an Unbelieving World

Published by Hendrickson Publishers
P. O. Box 3473
Peabody, Massachusetts 01961-3473

Printed in the United States of America

ISBN 1-56563-455-1

First printing—September 1999

Cover design by Sarah J. Slattery, Grand Rapids, Mich.
Interior design and typesetting by Pilcrow Book Services, Kirkland, Wash.
Edited by Judy Bodmer and Heather Stroobosscher

For the 3 Ks:

Kristyn, Kimberly, and Kaitlyn

May you find the greatness that God has put inside you!

CONTENTS

PREFACE

JESUS' SERMON on the Mount is an amazing summary of the best that human life can be and the means to find it. In fact, it seems almost foolish to write about the Sermon since there is nothing to add to a message that is so complete. To read through the entire Sermon, as I have done many times, is to come away exhilarated, anxious, and exhausted.

From the original listeners to readers today, exhilaration lifts all who marvel at the breadth of insight and common-sense spirituality that exudes from Jesus' words. This is no tedious doctrinal study; yet virtually the whole of Christian doctrine, apart from the specific story of Jesus' own atoning death, is found in these few chapters. The packaging, from beginning to end, is personal and challenging. As Jesus talks, we are able to picture faces of people we know. Often, in fact, we peer into the mirror of his words to find our own selves, stark without the makeup of our daily disguises. By the time we've moved from Jesus' blessing on those who find themselves infant strugglers in the Kingdom (the Beatitudes of Matthew 5) to his challenging altar call (in Matthew 7), we are caught up in something that is bigger than ourselves. We may have stumbled into the Kingdom, but we are not given the leisure to rest near the door.

Anxiety grips us as well. Jesus puts too many demands on us. None can be that strong, that spiritual, that good, that true, that honest, that constant. While breathing the life of God into us, he constantly remodels the house of our souls. There is pain in facing religion as pure and straight as this.

That is why, at the end, we crawl in exhaustion through the narrow gate and up the difficult way, having left behind in chapter 6 a lot of the things that we thought we needed for the trip. Even then, it is grace that leads us home, and not our own petty pride.

Reflecting on Jesus' words in the Sermon on the Mount took its toll on me. I think my life is the better for it, but the growth comes at a price. I hope I have captured my reflections in such a way that you will experience, as I did, the trauma of becoming transparent before God. More than that, I hope you will find, as I have, an even richer understanding of spirituality. The One who searches my life for authentic expressions of character and religion is also the One who says, "My grace is sufficient for you, for my power is made perfect in weakness."

As I write these words, the Lenten season begins. Jesus walked a difficult path. Perhaps we are getting better at walking it with him. And perhaps these words will help.

WAYNE BROUWER

Now when he saw the crowds, he went up on a mountainside and sat down. His disciples came to him, and he began to teach them, saying:

"Blessed are the poor in spirit,
for theirs is the kingdom of heaven.
"Blessed are those who mourn,
for they will be comforted.
"Blessed are the meek,
for they will inherit the earth.
"Blessed are those who hunger and thirst for righteousness,
for they will be filled.
"Blessed are the merciful,
for they will be shown mercy.
"Blessed are the pure in heart,
for they will see God.
"Blessed are the peacemakers,
for they will be called sons of God.
"Blessed are those who are persecuted because of righteousness,
for theirs is the kingdom of heaven.

"Blessed are you when people insult you, persecute you and falsely say all kinds of evil against you because of me. Rejoice and be glad, because great is your reward in heaven, for in the same way they persecuted the prophets who were before you."

—Matthew 5:1–12

1 WHEN GREATNESS FINDS ITSELF

Finding Your Identity Through the Crises of Life

FRED CRADDOCK TELLS of a vacation encounter in the Smokey Mountains of eastern Tennessee years ago that moved him deeply. He and his wife took supper one evening in a place called the Black Bear Inn. One side of the building was all glass, open to a magnificent mountain view. Glad to be alone, the Craddocks were a bit annoyed when an elderly man ambled over and struck up a nosey conversation: "Are you on vacation?" "Where are you from?" "What do you do?"

When he discovered that Fred taught in a seminary, the man suddenly had a preacher story to tell. "I was born back here in these mountains," he said. "My mother was not married, and her shame fell upon me. The children at school called me horrible names. During recess I would go hide in the weeds until the bell rang," he told Fred. "At lunchtime I took my lunch and went behind a tree to avoid them.

"Things got worse when I went to town. Men and women would stare at my mother and me, trying to guess the identity of my father. About seventh or eighth grade, I started to go hear a preacher. He wore a clawhammer tailcoat, striped trousers and had a face that looked like it had been quarried out of the mountain. He frightened me in a way, and he attracted me in a way. His voice thundered.

"I was afraid of what people would say to me, so I'd sneak into church just in time for the sermon, then rush out quickly when it was done. One Sunday, some women had cued up in the aisle and I couldn't get out and I began to get cold and sweaty and was sure that somebody would challenge me, 'What's a boy like you doing in church?'

"Suddenly I felt a hand on my shoulder. I looked out of the corner of my eye and saw that beard and saw that face. The minister stared at me and I thought, 'Oh, no. Oh, no. He's gonna guess.'

"The minister focused a penetrating glare at me and then said, 'Well boy, you're a child of ah . . . You're a child of ah . . . Ah, wait.' The preacher paused dramatically, getting ready to announce the horrible revelation to the whole church. Then he said, 'You're a child of God! I see a strikin' resemblance!'

"He swatted me on the bottom," said the old man, "and then told me, 'Go claim your inheritance, boy!'"

Fred Craddock looked more closely at the old man and asked, "What's your name?"

As the gentleman got up to wander on, he proudly replied, "Ben Hooper!" Fred remembered his own father telling him about the time when for two terms the people of Tennessee had elected an illegitimate governor named Ben Hooper. The outcast had survived. The shamed had succeeded. The boy of infamy was transformed into a man of fame and stature.

How does it happen? How does shame turn to self-assurance and guilt to grace? How did Ben Hooper, a child of social poverty, emerge as a leader of society?

Erik Erikson, the social analyst, said it happens when greatness finds itself. In fact, Erikson used that theme to describe the early years of another "nobody" who vaulted to world fame, the great reformer Martin Luther. Erikson reflected on what it was that made Luther a man who could change world history; his assessment was that in Luther, greatness found itself. Luther, he said, was someone who had the seeds of greatness within him, and through the circumstances of his life, he eventually found what it took to make a difference.

It can happen to anyone, said Dr. Erikson. Usually, however, the transition from ordinary existence to greatness happens when people are forced to endure three major crises of life and manage to face themselves honestly each time.

IDENTITY CRISIS

The first is the identity crisis. It's the crisis we face when we ask ourselves who we really are. Not just what this job has made us. Not just what Mom and Dad think we should be. Not just the roles we play with our friends, but who we really are. What it is that makes us special and different and unique among the billions of other bodies occupying space on planet earth.

Tony Campolo once told of a student who came to him in his office at Eastern Christian College. The young man explained to Dr. Campolo that he was going to take a semester off from college in order to travel for a while and get away from all the pressures that were consuming him. He said, "I don't know who I am anymore." Because of the expectations laid on him by his parents, his friends, his professors, and his girlfriend, he felt he had to get away from it all and find himself again.

Tony Campolo commended him. "That's a good thing to do!" he said. "But what if you start peeling away the layers of yourself, like an onion, and when you get rid of them you don't find anything at the center? What if you get to the heart of who you are, and you find there's nothing there? What do you do then?"

It's a tough question, one that most of us face at some point in our lives. Albert Camus wrote about that in his novel *The Fall*. A respected lawyer is walking the streets of Amsterdam one night. He hears a splash and then a cry for help. A woman has fallen into the canal! He begins to run toward the splashing. But then his legal mind whirls into action: Someone should help her, but should it be him? After all, he had his reputation to think about. What would people say if she were a prostitute, or even another man's wife, and their names appeared in the newspaper together? Or, worse yet, a picture of him helping her? Would they think he'd been with here? And what about his safety? Maybe some tough guys mugged her. Maybe they were still lingering in the shadows! Maybe they'd attack him, too, if he helped her!

He is deeply involved in his mental legal debate when suddenly he realizes that the splashing has stopped. The cries for help have ceased. The woman has drowned. The lawyer wanders on, still playing the arguments in his mind, deliberating whether or not he should have tried to save her. He stops at a tavern to drink himself into peace and uses the first person he can find as a father-confessor. Camus pronounces judgment on the lawyer in two short lines: "He did not answer the cry for help. That is the man he was."

We are each that person sometimes.

But now listen to Jesus again. "Blessed are those who mourn," he says. Why? Because those who are able to mourn have passed through a crisis of life. Because they have had to face the meaning of their lives and were forced to count the cost of things that matter. In the pain of giving up things they loved but didn't need, they find God's comfort.

In a parable by Kierkegaard, there was a break-in at a large store, but the thieves didn't take anything. When the clerks opened the store in the morning, all the merchandise was still there. What the thieves had done, however, was switch all the price tags. A diamond necklace was marked $2.00, and a pair of leather shoes, fifty cents. A pencil, however, now cost $75.00, and a baby's rattle was priced at $5000.

Instead of stealing merchandise, the thieves had stolen value. By stealing intrinsic worth, they had stolen *identity*. When the prices changed, no one knew any longer what the value was beneath the packaging.

Shelley Rodriguez, of Independence, Kentucky, explains the phenomenon this way. She brought her eight-year-old grandson to a farm. He loved the magic of the auctioneer's singsong voice, yet something bothered him. "Grandma!" he asked, "How's that man ever going to sell anything? He keeps changing the prices!"

Sometimes that seems to be the power of our society—changing the price tags on us, so we don't really know the value of things anymore.

Changing the price tags of our identity, so we don't really know who we are. "Blessed are the meek," says Jesus. But what's the value of meekness in our aggressive society? Do we really know? Do we know the value of ourselves? Do we really know who we are?

Levina Thiessen, of Winnipeg, Manitoba, remembers bringing the family out to watch her husband's city baseball team one summer. After the game, their three-year-old daughter raced out onto the ball diamond to find her father. The team was gathered in a post-game cluster, and since all the men wore the same uniform, the little girl was suddenly confounded. She looked back at her mom with tears in her eyes and yelled, "Mommy, which Daddy is mine?"

This is the crisis of identity. We're all trying to pretend, projecting more on the outside than we feel on the inside. In fact, sometimes the thing we're hiding most is something that's not even there—the emptiness of our own souls.

As one young woman put it, "Deep down, I'm shallow!" Maybe so. But shallowness is more than just a bent of character. It's a bent of no character. It's a mark of sin. That's why Jesus can say so forthrightly: "Blessed are those who are persecuted because of righteousness." No one persecutes a shallow person. Someone who is persecuted because of righteousness is a person who has an identity that others can respond to.

INFLUENCE CRISIS

That brings us to the second major crisis of life. Dr. Erikson calls it the influence crisis. What difference does my life make for others?

As parents, we want to influence our children. One pastor I know moved his family seven different times. During each of the last five moves, he left one or two children behind. Now, as he retires, he's trying to figure out what's become of his family, and what impact his life has had on his children. He mourns that the center is gone. They have no place to call home.

Parents make choices that affect the manner in which their children form their identities. Harry Chapin put it well in his song "Cat's in the

Cradle." When he was a young father, he was too busy making a living to take time with his son. When he was finally old enough to enjoy time with the family, his son in turn had learned to be too busy for his dad.

Of course, parents can have a positive influence, too. Maurice Boyd, a colleague of mine, remembers one incident that sealed the impact of his father on his life forever. His father worked in a shipyard in Belfast, Northern Ireland. During the Depression, work dried up. Times were tough, and for three years his father was out of a job.

Then one of his father's old bosses at the shipyard approached him. The important man would find work for Mr. Boyd. He would guarantee it, no matter how much worse things got. All Mr. Boyd would have to do would be to buy a life insurance policy from the man. It would work to their mutual benefit: the boss's income would increase, and Mr. Boyd's work income would be guaranteed!

It was a great deal except for one thing: it was illegal. Maurice Boyd remembers his father sitting at the kitchen table with the whole family surrounding him. There at the table his father counted the cost. He reviewed their desperate financial situation. He ticked off the outstanding bills and the money he could be making, *ought* to be making, if only he'd say yes to his boss.

His father wrote it all down on a sheet of paper: the gains and the losses, what he could make and what he could lose. Then he wrote down a category that Maurice Boyd will never forget: integrity. What did it matter if he gained the cash to pay the rent, but lost his ability to teach his children right from wrong? What did it matter if he gained the dignity of a job but lost it each morning when he looked at himself in the mirror and knew that the only one reason he could go off to work instead of someone else was because he cheated?

His father declined the job, and the family groveled through several more years of poverty. Yet, of his father, Maurice Boyd says, "He discovered that no one can make you feel inferior without your consent, and that one way you can keep your soul is by refusing to sell it. He realized that whatever else he lost . . . he didn't have to lose himself."

Jesus put it this way: "Blessed are the pure in heart, for they will see God." So will their children.

Yet it isn't a formula that we can play out in our lives through some program or recipe. Robert Coles, child psychiatrist and Harvard University professor, tried at one time to figure out why we do the things we do. In his book *The Call of Service,* Coles reflects on people who try to make a difference in life. People who seek to reform themselves, even when sinful tendencies oozed like tentacles through their inner marrow. People who attempt to better society, in spite of the fact that it stubbornly refuses the challenge.

Why do they do it? Coles asks. The people themselves often have a hard time defining what makes them tick. One young teacher in an urban school gets challenged all the time by street-smart students. Weary of self-righteous do-gooders, they ask, "What's in it for you?" And he really can't say.

But all these compassionate volunteers have one thing in common: earlier in their lives, each of them ran into a crisis situation that tested their identity and their willingness to do something about it. In that crisis situation, each of them encountered someone who put his or her life on the line and taught them the meaning of service. Someone who gave of themselves in a way that bucks the trend of selfishness and of self-preservation. And the influence of that someone else made it possible for the person they helped to be greater than each of them had previously thought they could be.

Greatness finding itself. Do you see it? In a troubled world, says Jesus, where the safest bet is self-preservation, "Blessed are the peacemakers, for they will be called children of God." Do you see them around you? Do you know the names of some whose last name is Father, and Son, and Holy Spirit? Do you know any "children of God"? Then you've been touched by greatness finding itself.

CRISIS OF INTEGRITY

The third crisis of life Dr. Erikson talks about is the crisis of integrity.

Why is Jesus so big on persecution? Why does he say so sharply and so powerfully: "Blessed are you when people insult you, persecute you, and falsely say all kinds of evil against you because of me"?

For one simple reason: the hardest thing to do in life is to maintain your integrity. Sin has entered the human soul precisely at this point. We're rather nice, aren't we? There's much that we do that's good and fine and noble and kind and wise, and no one can deny that.

But here's the problem: whatever else sin might do in our lives, it first and foremost perforates the lines of the heart, and lets us tear off a piece here and a piece there, till we find ourselves fragmented, torn apart in separate snippets of self. It isn't that we become blackened by sin in large strokes. It isn't that we turn into hideous monsters of greed and cruelty. It isn't that we dissolve the Dr. Jekylls of our personalities into dastardly Mr. Hydes. Rather, we keep most of our goodness intact, while making small allowances here and there. We cheat on our taxes a little, maybe. Or we turn our eyes from the needs of someone we could help. Or we compromise our communication till we speak from only our mouths instead of our souls.

The fragmentation of our lives makes us less than we should be, less than we could be. It makes us less than the people God made us to be.

There is a powerful scene in Robert Bolt's play *A Man for All Seasons*. The story is about Sir Thomas More, loyal subject of the English crown. King Henry VIII wants to change things to suit his own devious plans, so he requires all his nobles to swear an oath of allegiance which violates the conscience of Sir Thomas More before his God. Since he will not swear the oath, More is put in jail. His daughter Margaret comes to visit him. Meg, he calls her, with affection. She's his pride and joy, the one who thinks his thoughts after him.

Meg comes to plead with her father in prison. "Take the oath, Father!" she urges him. "Take it with your mouth, if you can't take it with your heart! Take it and return to us! You can't do us any good in here! And you can't be there for us if the king should execute you!"

She's right in so many ways. Yet her father answers her this way: "Meg, when a man swears an oath, he holds himself in his hands like water, and if he opens his fingers, how can he hope to find himself again?"

You know what he means, don't you? When our lives begin to fragment, it's like holding our lives like water in our hands, and then letting our fingers come apart, just a little bit. The water of our very selves dribbles away. We may look like the same people, but who we are inside has begun to change.

"Blessed are the pure in heart," says Jesus, and we know what he means. He means that we're all of a piece. There's no separation in us between the impulse of the heart and the thought of the mind and the word of the mouth and the action of the hands. Somehow, everything that we are is integrated. That's the meaning of the word integrity, isn't it? Pure in heart.

When Bill Moyers interviewed Dr. Rachel Naomi Remen, she told him how it was for her. Dr. Remen has founded several institutes for the care of cancer patients. She said that sometimes she has a much greater sense of integrity within herself during those times when she isn't feeling all that well physically. Bill asked her what she meant by integrity, and she replied, "That I am what I am. . . . " She said that even with her wounds and her weaknesses, "there's an essence and a uniqueness and a beauty" about her life that is whole and complete. Integrity—pure in heart.

Years ago, when radio station WXYZ in Detroit was the big news in broadcasting, people spent hours each night listening to the latest episodes of *The Green Hornet* and *Sergeant Preston of the Yukon*. Nearly every year the station brought out a new dramatic hero.

Station manager George Trendle often suggested the ideas for these characters. In fact, he was the inspiration behind one of the most famous figures they created: The Lone Ranger. Trendle said this about the man he had in mind: "He's a sober-minded man with a righteous purpose. Make kids look up to him." Greatness finding itself. Pure in heart.

But that's easily lost on us. When Thomas Naylor was teaching business management at Duke University, he asked his students to draft a personal strategic plan. He reports that "with few exceptions, what they wanted fell into three categories: money, power, and things—very big things."

In fact, said Naylor, this was their request of the business faculty at Duke University: "Teach me to be a money-making machine." A machine has no heart! That's the fragmentation of our lives taken to the extreme.

CONCLUSION

The beauty of life, though, is that each day we have a chance to start over. In some sense we are always on the brink of another year. It is said, "Today is the first day of the rest of your life." Let's imagine that there are 365 new days thrown back onto the credit side of the ledger. What do we do with them? We know the law of averages. Those who tally our demographic lives tell us that each day 9,077 babies are born; 2,740 young people run away from home; 63,288 traffic accidents occur, in which 129 people die; 5,962 couples get married and 1,986 divorce; 500 million cups of coffee are consumed; and the snack bars at O'Hare Airport in Chicago sell 5,479 hot dogs.

And each of us is challenged in one of the three great crises of life:

- *The Identity Crisis:* Who am I?
- *The Influence Crisis:* What does my life mean to those around me?
- *The Integrity Crisis:* How deep is my soul?

Perhaps, because we remember the words of Jesus, the method to our madness will change. Perhaps a new motto will guide us:

> "Blessed are the poor in spirit,
> for theirs is the kingdom of heaven.
> "Blessed are those who mourn,
> for they will be comforted.
> "Blessed are the meek,
> for they will inherit the earth.
> "Blessed are those who hunger and thirst for righteousness,
> for they will be filled.

"Blessed are the merciful,
for they will be shown mercy.
"Blessed are the pure in heart,
for they will see God.
"Blessed are the peacemakers,
for they will be called [children] of God.
"Blessed are those who are persecuted because of righteousness,
for theirs is the kingdom of heaven." (Matthew 5:3–10)

Of course, if that happens, we may change the color of society. After all, remember Martin Luther? Remember what happens when greatness begins to find itself? The world is never the same again!

"You are the salt of the earth. But if the salt loses its saltiness, how can it be made salty again? It is no longer good for anything, except to be thrown out and trampled by men.

"You are the light of the world. A city on a hill cannot be hidden. Neither do people light a lamp and put it under a bowl. Instead they put it on its stand, and it gives light to everyone in the house. In the same way, let your light shine before men, that they may see your good deeds and praise your Father in heaven.

—Matthew 5:13–16

2
DOES ANYBODY NOTICE?

Would the Neighborhood Look Different Without Followers of Christ?

THERE IS AN ancient legend first told by Christians living in the catacombs under the streets of Rome. It pictures the day when Jesus went back to glory after finishing all his work on earth. The angel Gabriel meets Jesus in heaven and welcomes him home. "Lord," Gabriel asks, "Who have you left behind to carry on your work?"

Jesus tells him about the disciples, the little band of fishermen and farmers and housewives.

"But Lord," says Gabriel, "what if they fail you? What if they lose heart or drop out? What if things get too rough for them and they let you down?"

"Well," says Jesus, "then all I've done will come to nothing."

"But don't you have a backup plan?" Gabriel asks. "Isn't there something else to keep it going, to finish your work?"

"No," says Jesus, "there's no backup plan. The church is it. There's nothing else."

"Nothing else?" asks Gabriel. "But what if they fail?"

And the early Christians knew Jesus' answer. "Gabriel," Jesus explained patiently, "They won't fail."

Isn't that a marvelous thing? Here are the Christians of Rome, dug into the earth like gophers, tunneling out of sight because of the terrors of

Nero up above. They're nothing in that world. They're poor and despised and insignificant. Yet they know the promise of Jesus: "You won't fail. You're my people, and you won't fail."

That's what Jesus tells us in these verses, doesn't he? "You are the salt of the earth," he says. "You are the light of the world. You are my witnesses."

There are four things that Jesus is saying to us when he gives us that testimony.

YOU CAN MAKE A DIFFERENCE

The first is this: "You can make a difference." You can make a difference in the world around you.

Think of the crowd to which Jesus was speaking. It wasn't a gathering of the United Nations. It wasn't a conference of the superpowers. It wasn't a sitting of congress or parliament or even an assembly at city hall. It was a crowd on a hillside in a tiny spot of land called Palestine. It was a group of common people with no high ambitions or positions. In fact, they were under occupation. They couldn't make their own laws. They couldn't plan their own futures. They couldn't determine their own destinies. Yet Jesus says to them, "*You* are the salt of the earth. *You* are the light of the world. *You* make a difference in this society." It's an amazing assertion, isn't it?

We are tempted to pass over the small and insignificant in society, dismissing them casually. Tony Campolo told of his friend who was walking through the midway at a county fair when he met a tiny girl. She was carrying a great big fluff of cotton candy on a stick, almost as large as herself. He said to her, "How can a little girl like you eat all that cotton candy?"

"Well," she said to him, "I'm really much bigger on the inside than I am on the outside!"

That's essentially what Jesus is saying here: "You are the salt of the earth. You are the light of the world." Why? Because of your great power? Because of your positions in government? Because you are so smart or so strong or so gifted? "No," Jesus would say. "It's because you belong to me." On the outside you may seem to be nothing, but on the inside you're as big as the Kingdom and the power and the glory of your God. You can make a difference.

Rallying against the usual helplessness of our mediocre days are stories of courage that remind us of the truth of Jesus' word. There's a marvelous little story tucked away in the pages of Edward Gibbon's seven-volume work *The Decline and Fall of the Roman Empire*. It tells about a humble little monk named Telemachus living in the farming regions of Asia.

Telemachus had no great ambitions in life. He loved his little garden and tilled it through the changing seasons. But one day in A.D. 391 he felt a sense of urgency, a call of God's direction in his life. He didn't know why, but he felt that God wanted him to go to Rome, the heart and soul of the empire. In fact, the feelings of such a call frightened him, but he went anyway, praying along the way for God's direction.

When he finally got to the city, it was in an uproar. The armies of Rome had just come home from the battlefield in victory, and the crowds were turning out for a great celebration. They flowed through the streets like a tidal wave, and Telemachus was caught in their frenzy and carried into the Coliseum.

Down in the arena men hacked at each other with swords and clubs. He had never seen a gladiator contest before, but now his heart sickened. The crowds roared at the sight of blood and urged their favorites on to the death.

Telemachus couldn't stand it. He knew it was wrong; this wasn't the way God wanted people to live or to die. So little Telemachus worked his way through the crowds to the wall down by the arena. "In the name of Christ, forbear!" he shouted.

Nobody heard him, so he crawled up onto the wall and shouted again: "In the name of Christ, forbear!" This time the few who heard him only laughed. But Telemachus was not to be ignored. He jumped into the arena and ran through the sands toward the gladiators. "In the name of Christ, forbear!"

The crowds laughed at the silly little man and threw stones at him. Telemachus, however, was on a mission. He threw himself between two gladiators to stop their fighting. "In the name of Christ, forbear!" he cried.

They hacked him apart. They cut his body from shoulder to stomach, and he fell onto the sand with the lifeblood running out of him.

The gladiators were stunned, and they stopped to watch him die. Then the crowds fell back in silence, and, for a moment, no one in the Coliseum moved. Telemachus' final words rang in their memories: "In the name of Christ, forbear!" At last they moved, slowly at first, but growing in numbers. The masses of Rome filed out of the Coliseum that day, and the historian Theodoret reports that never again was a gladiator contest held there. All because of the witness and the testimony of a single Christian.

"*You* are the salt of the earth! *You* are the light of the world!" You can make a difference in life.

YOU CAN MAKE A DIFFERENCE TOGETHER

You can make a difference. But Jesus adds a second thing to it. We can make a difference *together.*

"If the salt loses its saltiness, how can it be made salty again?" asks Jesus. "It's good for nothing, and you throw it out into the streets."

Is it possible for salt to become unsalty?

Not really. Any chemistry teacher will tell you that. Sodium chloride is one of the most stable compounds in the whole of the universe. It doesn't change. It doesn't lose its character.

Still, there is truth to what Jesus is saying. Much of the salt used in Palestine came from the area around the Dead Sea, which, at more than a mile and a half *below* sea level, is the lowest land area in the world. The waters of the Sea of Galilee flow into the Jordan River and from there to the Dead Sea, the bottom of the earth. Once they get there, it's the end of the line. There's no place to go. The hot desert sun evaporates the water and leaves behind a chunky white powder made up of a combination of salts and minerals.

That powder contains enough salt to season meat or to add a little flavor to soup. For that reason the people of Palestine have always scooped it up to use in trade and in cooking. But the salt is mixed with minerals. It's not pure sodium chloride. Indeed, it is possible, under certain circumstances, with a little dampness in the air, for the salts to be dissolved first and leached away.

What you have left looks the same, yet the taste is gone, and people throw it out. There may be a little salt left, but it isn't enough to make a difference, so the whole batch is chucked out into the street.

The comparison point Jesus makes, in essence, is that strength is found in community. A single grain of salt may make a slight difference, but it takes a multiplication of granules working together to make a real impact. Similarly, one disciple with a sense of purpose may make a statement in the world, but it's the community of Christians that turns the world upside down.

We saw that in Romania during the days when Communism was coming undone. One Christian preacher spoke to his congregation, giving testimony to the grace of God that had changed their lives. He urged them to work together to change their country. Then he was shot, struck down by the powers of the governing authority. But his people became a community of salt and light. They flowed from the doors of that church building and carried the crusade into the streets. They challenged the powers that sat in repressive authority and demanded freedoms for decent living.

The community made an impact. Others felt the leavening influence of it in the streets. The community of the church salted Romanian society, and it got a fresh taste, a different outlook, and a new character.

We, *together,* are the salt of the earth. We, *together,* are the light of the world. Not just a lonely grain of sodium chloride, but the tablespoon that spreads its essence through the whole pot of soup.

It's hard sometimes to imagine just how important community is. We like to think of ourselves as independent and strong, full of personal vitality. Yet often the first thing we hear from the lips of someone who is experiencing problems is, "Nobody cares. I'm all alone."

Some time ago I sat at a table with old friends. Years before they were the strongest Christians I knew. They loved the Lord; they loved their church; they were full of enthusiasm.

But this night, they were different. They were hurting and confused. They felt weak and tired spiritually. Why? Their congregation was torn apart, they said, and the people they sat next to in church were fighting one another. Their community had become a battleground.

My friends are still Christians, but their oldest son has stopped going to church with them. They have to drag the younger ones along, and they've backed out of many ministry commitments that had meant so much to them in the past.

The community is gone, and with it went the power. The strength of their Christianity in testimony and witness has disappeared. When they talk about it, they sound tired. They can't be salt anymore. They can't light up their world. They're alone and slowly dying spiritually.

We can make a difference. But like the flicker of a thousand lights in the city on the hill, or the powerful taste of a spoonful of salt in the potatoes, we can do that best *together*—as a community.

YOU CAN MAKE A DIFFERENCE TOGETHER IN THE WORLD

There's a third thing that Jesus tells us in the words, we can make a difference. We can make a difference together *in the world*.

I'm captivated by the events that surrounded the start of my own denomination, the Christian Reformed Church. One of our first pastors, the Rev. H. G. Kleijn, sent a letter to a Classis Holland meeting on April 8, 1857, telling the other church leaders that he was pulling out to start a new denomination. The church they were part of, he said, had too many contacts with the world around it. The church should be off by itself, separated from the rest of society, living its own little life in its own little corner. Here are his words: "The Church, the Bride of Christ, is a garden enclosed, a well shut up, and a fountain sealed."

Thankfully our denomination has gone well beyond the isolation of its early years and developed a strong evangelical witness. But Rev. Kleijn's view of the church has often intrigued me. Do you see his picture? The Church is a nice little community off by itself, doing its own thing, untouched by the world. It's as pretty as a garden full of flowers, but it puts a high wall around itself so nobody else can get in. It's a well of refreshing water, but stopped up so nobody will get it dirty by taking a drink. It's a fountain of surging excitement, albeit sealed within concrete barriers so its power won't slip away. That's the church Rev. Kleijn said he wanted to belong to.

But that doesn't seem to be the church that Jesus envisions. Besides the power of flavor, there was an even greater strength of salt in the world of Jesus' day. Salt was used to confirm agreements, to seal treaties and establish covenants. If you ate salt with someone, you became blood relatives. You had a stake in each other's lives. You were part of the same family.

King Abijah, in the Old Testament, reminds the people that they made a "treaty of salt" with David, and therefore they can't break it. The enemies of the Jews, in the book of Ezra, write a letter to King Artaxerxes of Persia, telling him that they will be his servants forever because they have eaten salt from his treasuries. They are his servants, confirmed by eating his salt.

In Arabic, the word for salt is the same word as the word for treaty. Similarly, in Persian, the word for traitor means someone who is faithless to salt. Not that many years ago this was all proved again in the modern state of Jordan. Informants for the King uncovered an assassination plot and reported to him the name of the man who was supposed to kill him.

In response, the King devised and ingenious plan. Rather than sending his soldiers out to arrest the man, foiling the plot with guns and weapons, he invited the traitor to the royal palace for a dinner. Since it is impossible to refuse a royal invitation, the man was obligated to enter the territory of his target.

The King made certain that the meal was heavily salted. At that point things changed. Once they had eaten salt together there was a bond between them. The assassin became a brother, and he couldn't kill the King.

Such a picture resonates with what Jesus gives us here. "You are the salt of the earth," he says. You are the essence of God's relationship with the world around you. The Church isn't just a little community off by itself somewhere. It is the confirmation that God still has an interest in our world.

The Old Testament story of Lot and his family is instructive. Sodom was a wicked place; so wicked, in fact, that God *had* to destroy it. "Enough is enough!" he must have said to himself.

But before he destroyed Sodom, he came down to earth and talked his plans over with Abraham. Lot was Abraham's nephew, and God wanted to make certain that Abraham understood what was going on. After they talked about it for awhile, Abraham said to God, "I hear what you're saying. I know it's a wicked place. I agree, something's got to be done. But what if there are fifty good people there? Would you still destroy it, even with fifty good people living there?"

"No," said God, "I wouldn't. If there are only fifty good people living in Sodom, I'll spare the whole city."

Abraham got his courage up. "But what if there aren't quite fifty good people there? What if you go down and count them, and you find only forty-five? Would you still destroy the city?"

"No," said God, "I reckon not. If there are only forty-five good people there, I won't bring down my judgment on the place."

Abraham was on a roll now. He decided to press his luck. "Would you spare it for the sake of thirty righteous people?"

God probably sighed, but then he said, "I guess I'd go that far."

In the end Abraham asked again about twenty, and about ten, and God agreed to his terms. If only ten righteous people lived in Sodom, God would spare the whole city. The meaning is clear: the viability of a neighborhood is somehow tied to the residual influence of those who have a meaningful connection with God.

In the New Testament the apostle Peter picks up that same theme. He says there is enough evil in society, enough wickedness in our world for God to let loose the fires of his judgment. But he's not going to do that yet, says Peter, because he has people living throughout the whole wide world, and they make a difference. They confirm God's relationship with his world. They are the salt of the earth.

What would your city be without your testimony? What would your region be like without the Church of Jesus Christ? Where would your nation be without the conscience of the people of God? "You are the salt of the earth," says Jesus. "You are the light of the world." You are not to hide in a corner. You are not to hug yourself within the walls of your pretty little garden. You are not to keep off by yourself, hoping nobody notices you.

"You are the light of the world." It's not enough to be anti-abortion; you must be pro-life and remind your community what real life, God's life, is all about. It's not enough to be against immorality; you have to be the conscience of society, turning its thoughts toward love and laughter and life. It's not enough to protect your own interests; you have to speak out for the welfare of the poor, the disabled, the oppressed.

"You are the salt of the earth." You are the conscience of your society. God has placed us here as a symbol of his continuing relationship with his world. We are the extension of his personality in this society. What difference does it make that we're here? Does anybody notice?

YOU CAN MAKE A DIFFERENCE TOGETHER IN THE WORLD FOR GOD

And, finally, we can make a difference together in the world *for God*.

It's not enough to be socially active, socially responsible, socially concerned. "Let your light shine before men," says Jesus here, "that they may see your good deeds and praise your Father in heaven!" Turn people's thoughts toward God. No mind is truly enlightened until it is flooded with the glory of heaven. No body is truly healed until it is touched by the power of the Creator. No person is truly set free until there is freedom of the Spirit of Christ.

William Carey was a pastor of a small congregation in Leiceter, England. In 1792 he preached a powerful sermon called "Expect Great Things from God; Attempt Great Things for God." People would remember it for years. His message not only moved hearts in his congregation, it also came home to challenge Pastor Carey's own soul. The next year he set sail for India, and what he did in that country was simply astounding. He began a manufacturing plant to employ jobless workers. He translated the scriptures and set up shops to print them. He established schools for all ages, helping people find a better place in society. He provided medical assistance for the diseased and the troubled and the ailing. He was nothing short of a miracle for the people of India.

Why did he do it? Because Jesus told him, "You are the salt of the earth. You are the light of the world." And when he lay dying, these were his last words: "When I have gone, speak not of Carey but of Carey's Savior."

There was only one reason for it all: ". . . that they may see your good deeds, and glorify your Father in heaven"

You can make a difference in the world for God.

During the time of the Reformation, John Foxe of England was impressed by the testimony of the early Christians. He gleaned the pages of early historical writings and wrote a book that has become a classic in the church: *Foxe's Book of Martyrs*.

One story he tells is about an early church leader named Lawrence. Lawrence acted as a pastor for a church community. He also collected the offerings for the poor each week, and that led to his death.

A band of thieves found out that Lawrence received the offerings of the people from Sunday to Sunday, so one night, as he was out taking a stroll, they grabbed him and demanded the money. He told them that he didn't have it. He had already given it all to the poor. They didn't believe him and told him they would give him a chance to find it. In three days they would come to his house and take from him the treasures of the church.

Three days later they did come. But Lawrence wasn't alone. The house was filled with the people of his congregation. When the thieves demanded the treasure of the church, Lawrence smiled. He opened wide his arms and gestured to those who sat around him. "Here's the treasure of the church," he said. "Here's the treasure of God that shines in the world."

We are the salt of the earth. We are the light of the world. We can make a difference together in the world for God.

"Do not think that I have come to abolish the Law or the Prophets; I have not come to abolish them but to fulfill them. I tell you the truth, until heaven and earth disappear, not the smallest letter, not the least stroke of a pen, will by any means disappear from the Law until everything is accomplished. Anyone who breaks one of the least of these commandments and teaches others to do the same will be called least in the kingdom of heaven, but whoever practices and teaches these commands will be called great in the kingdom of heaven. For I tell you that unless your righteousness surpasses that of the Pharisees and the teachers of the law, you will certainly not enter the kingdom of heaven."

—Matthew 5:17–20

3
"ON BEYOND" PERFECTION

Grace Beyond the Daily Grind of Being Nice

TWENTY-SIX LETTERS might be good enough for most people, but for Dr. Seuss, that's just the beginning. In his book *On Beyond Zebra*, one of his great little characters takes the reader on a tour of life beyond "Z is for Zebra." It's a whole new world of creatures most of us have never seen before. Things run on different time schedules, and life itself has a very different feel about it in the world *On Beyond Zebra*.

Jesus does something similar in Matthew 5:17–20. The whole of the Sermon on the Mount is about living life in the right way. It's about ethics and morality and about the kind of people we should be. That is why Jesus talks about the Law and the Prophets. For the people of his time, the laws of the Old Testament, and the prophets who interpreted them, were the standard by which you judged right and wrong.

Think of it like this: your friend tells you that she's cutting a class and sneaking out to the beach for an hour. What do you say? "Hey, I'm coming with you!" Or maybe, "Do you think we'll get away with it? Do you think we'll get caught?"

You see, there's some standard by which you judge your actions. Maybe it's by the rules of the school. Maybe it's by the laws laid down by your parents. There is always some norm by which we judge our actions—Is it right? Is it legal? Will I get away with it?

For the people of Jesus' day, it was the Law and the Prophets of the Old Testament. The rules and regulations of the Hebrew scriptures told people how to live.

Most people thought these were enough. Take the Pharisees and the scribes, for instance. The law and the prophets were enough for them. That was how they regulated their lives. They felt no need for anything more.

When Jesus said he had come to fulfill the Law and the Prophets, I'll bet the people's faces brightened: "Hey, this Jesus isn't all bad. He's sticking with the way we've always done things. What a relief. Most of the young teachers nowadays are becoming far too liberal. Good thing this Jesus embraces conservative values."

But Jesus didn't tread lightly on those religious leaders. In fact, Jesus went on to say some pretty harsh things. "I tell you," he said, "unless your righteousness *surpasses* that of the Pharisees and the teachers of the law, you will certainly not enter the kingdom of heaven."

Wow! What does Jesus mean by that statement? The Pharisees were trying to live perfect lives. What kind of demands is Jesus painting for us in the land on beyond perfection?

WE GO BEYOND SAYING YES TO UNDERSTANDING NO

One of the things that Jesus is saying to us is this: in the land on beyond perfection, we go beyond merely saying yes to understanding the meaning of no.

Our daughters are perfect examples of that. No matter how fast they are growing up, it's never fast enough for them. They see adults, and they think that we have it so good. They can't *wait* to be grown up so that life will be wonderful for them too.

What is it that makes adults' lives seem so wonderful? It's probably a combination of a number of things, but most important among those is this—they think that *we* can do so many more things than *they* can. We can stay up later. We can watch whatever programs we want to on television. We can drive cars and go wherever we want. When we go to the grocery store, we can buy whatever we wish, even all the junk food we can pile in the cart.

There are so many things that we can do as adults that they can't. They have to go to bed on time. They have to practice piano. They have to go to school. They can't eat just anything they want.

They look at us and think that it must be *wonderful* to be an adult. To be able to say yes to so many fun things in life. And they know that someday, when they grow up, they'll be able to do *anything* they want to do. Right?

Wrong.

When you finally grow up and at last have the legal right to do anything you want, life itself changes you. Other kinds of laws take over. Maybe your parents won't say "no" to you anymore, and maybe even the laws of the government won't stop you from doing some things. But you begin to learn that the only true way to say yes to anything in life is by learning how to say no to something else.

Sure, you can eat anything you want. That also means, however, that you can't wear the clothes you used to wear. Sure, you can stay up as late as you want. But that also dictates that you can't do other things you might have thought about doing the next morning. Sure, you can have sexual relationships with as many people as you can get into your bed, but the other side of that truth is that you can't have intimacy with anybody.

Somehow, the quality of our lives is found as much in our ability to understand the meaning of no as it is in our wonderful capacity to say yes. I once asked a pastor that I've known for many years how things were going for him in his retirement.

"Wayne," he said to me, "I've never enjoyed life so much. I'm just as busy now as I used to be, but it's different. I found this wonderful little word that I'd forgotten how to use. It's the little word spelled 'N-O'."

He went on to say, "I'm finding out just who I am again, because I'm learning how to use the word *no*."

During the Middle Ages theologians used to debate questions like how many angels can dance on the head of a pin, or where does the soul come from when a child is born, or can God create a stone too big for him to move?

While those issues may be interesting diversions, the problem with such inquiries is that they forget that this is a moral universe. The question is not whether God can do something bigger than God can control, but whether God will do something which is outside of God's moral character.

You see, there are some things God *can* do, because God is God, but he *won't* do, precisely for the same reason: because God is God. When God says to you, "I have loved you with and everlasting love. I will always be there for you. You can count on me. I will never leave you or forsake you," then God is saying yes to you in letters as big as the heavens. But God is also saying, "No, I will not let the evil in this world grab hold of you forever. I will not allow even death to snatch you away from me. Never. No matter what may happen, child, I'll never let go of your hand."

That's why Jesus says that he didn't come to destroy the Law and the Prophets. The Law and the Prophets were God's way of hanging onto his people. They were the powerful no to sin and evil and death that framed the great yes of God's love for us.

So when Jesus wants us to travel with him to a land on beyond perfection, he's reminding us that no great yes is ever shaped apart from its line of definition.

Who are you? You know it by the lines you draw.

WE GO BEYOND LEGALISM TO LIBERTY

Learning the meaning of no isn't enough. A cartoon ran in *The New Yorker* some time ago. The scene shows a man at the gate of heaven. He's just died, and now he's carrying on a nervous conversation with the apostle Peter. There are beads of perspiration running down the man's face. He's wringing his hands in anxiety as he tries to give a good account of his life.

Peter, however, is shaking his head. "No, no, no!" he says. "That's not a sin either! My goodness! You must have worried yourself to death!"

The morality of Jesus is more than just lines of definition. The tough part of what Jesus says is this: "Unless your righteousness surpasses that of the Pharisees and the teachers of the law, there isn't a place for you in the kingdom of heaven."

Who were these Pharisees and teachers of the law?

They've gotten pretty poor press over the years. Nobody seems to think anything good about Pharisees. Just look at the stories in the Gospels. A Pharisee goes up to the Temple to pray. He stands up there in all his pride and thanks God that he's not an ugly, sniveling creature like that despicable tax collector over there.

Or think of the time that Simon the Pharisee invites Jesus to his house for dinner, only he forgets to have Jesus' feet washed at the door. He forgets to treat Jesus with respect, and he laughs about Jesus' acquaintances to his friends sitting at the table. You get the idea that Pharisees were rather rude people.

Later, when you find out that they were in on the plot to kill Jesus, it doesn't polish up the picture we have of them too much, does it?

But let's dig into the history books and find out a little more about these strange people. The first book we turn to is the rest of the New Testament. Who was the apostle Paul before he became a Christian? He was a Pharisee. And he tells us that being a Pharisee meant two things to him: a godly lifestyle and a belief in the resurrection.

In fact, when he was on trial one time, and they asked him what he believed, he looked at the Pharisees in the room and said he was still one of them. He still believed the things they believed, while he was already a Christian. Paul could be a Christian and a Pharisee at the same time. Pharisees were good people.

When we turn to the writings of Flavius Josephus, we get a similar picture. Josephus was the great historian of the Jewish people at the same time that the New Testament was being written. Josephus tells us about Pilate and Herod and even mentions Jesus a couple times. He also tries to explain to the Roman rulers the contours of Jewish society—who's who and what's what. When he mentions the Pharisees, he says that they were the best of Jewish people.

Indeed, he says that when he was a young man he personally lived for a time with each of the major groups within Jewish society: the Sadducees who cared for the Temple; the Essenes, who lived pure and separate lives out in the wilderness; and the Pharisees. Guess what? Josephus became a Pharisee and remained one for the rest of his life. Whenever he talks about the Pharisees, his words glow. He considered the Pharisees beautiful people. They cared about others. They cared about the quality of life. They were not rich, most of them, but they were wealthy in the things that mattered.

The Pharisees, Josephus writes, tried to live as God's people in all things. All of Jewish society looked up to them.

When you read Paul and Josephus, and their contemporary, Philo of Alexandria, you get a rather nice view of the Pharisees. In fact, if you try to translate that picture into today's world and the Christian church, this is the kind of person you might find calling himself a Pharisee:

He'd have grown up in a poor but pious home.

His parents would have sacrificed to send him to a private Christian school.

He'd be married, with children, and they'd have devotions together at mealtime.

Every week they'd attend worship together, and he'd serve a second term on the church council.

He would sacrifice to send his children to Christian schools.

His wife would be a volunteer at the local chapter of Right to Life.

He would attend Promise Keepers meetings and conventions.

He and his wife would listen to *Focus on the Family*.

As a family they'd support a Third World child through Compassion.

They'd contribute a tithe of all their income to the church.

Every year at least one week of vacation would be spent volunteering in some mission project.

That's what a Pharisee would look like today. Why, then, does Jesus have such a dim view of the Pharisees?

Actually, he probably doesn't. But Jesus knows whenever people begin to live good lives, there is a danger that they will start realizing it. That is the moment when whatever is morally upright in their lives becomes skewed and twisted and ugly. The danger of that happening is greater for nice people.

I had a friend at college who I thought was a great person with his head screwed on straight. He was one of the most genuine and caring persons I'd ever met. So it was quite a thrill when after graduation we both found summer jobs in Sioux Center, Iowa. We located two more roommates and rented a house from one of our professors who was going to be out of the country for the summer.

There we were, living together, going to ball games, sitting out on the porch on those lazy summer evenings, shooting the bull. But it almost killed our friendship. I thought so much of him that when we became housekeepers together, sharing so much time together, I told myself, Mark is an awfully good guy, and I think a lot of him. I'd better be on my best behavior. I don't want him to get upset with me.

Meanwhile, Mark was thinking the same thing about me. So here we were, two friends, and yet we were dancing this little dance around each other: "Whatever you like." "Sure, I'll do that for you!" "Oh, don't worry about it." "Just let me know if I can help you!" While we were looking at how to be nice, we forgot how to be real. When we forgot about being real with each other, we lost the very thing that made our earlier friendship so special.

That's the problem for *good* people. Once they grow in their goodness, it's easy for them to begin to focus on being good.

Professor Ed Dowey of Princeton Seminary showed how easy it is to slip from grace to legalism. He remembered strolling down a street one day, preoccupied with his own thoughts. Suddenly a young girl met him and gave him a smile so bright he couldn't help but feel the warmth and energy she brought into his world. He didn't know her and there was no other reason for them to connect except that they shared the sidewalk together. "It was a moment of grace," he said.

But then a funny thing happened. The next day he happened to be on that sidewalk again and he now found himself looking ahead at faces pushing toward him to see if that same young girl might come his way this day as well. Yes! There she was again! Immediately, said Dowey, something changed inside of him. Without thinking he edged toward her path before she even knew he was there. Then, as soon as she caught sight of him he shot her a huge smile and a friendly greeting. He still didn't know her, he said, but it seemed like the thing he had to do.

When he reflected on the incident later it occurred to him—what had been a moment of serendipitous grace the first day had captured his desire like a sweet treat. The second day he maneuvered to make it happen again. Rather than waiting to receive some little blessing from a stranger, he now tried to influence the circumstances in order to coerce another smile. The grin he received the first day was grace, commented Dowey, but the one he earned through manipulation on the second became a kind of legalism. To all outside appearances the actions were entirely unchanged from one day to the next. Inside, however, Dowey said, something had altered. He had tried to take a good thing and then buy it back again to recapture the feeling.

The morality of the world on beyond the perfection of the Pharisees and other nice people, says Jesus, is a morality that somehow manages to go beyond legalism to liberty. In other words, it's a morality that remembers that the other *person* is more important than the day to day *activities* of our relationship. If I love my wife, Brenda, I should talk with her, spend time with her, do nice things for her, protect her, and plan evenings with her.

But it's also possible for me to talk with Brenda and to spend time with her and to do nice things for her and to protect her and to plan activities with her and yet, at the same time, to let the meaning of our relationship slip away.

So it is in our relationship with God. The harshest words Jesus had were directed at "good people," like the Pharisees. Do not take his words lightly . The people furthest from the Kingdom of God are those who seem most to have it in hand.

Listen to what Mike Yaconelli, a pastor, said in an interview: "Commitment is a fine word—in most contexts. But as a religious word, a word that defines my faith . . . well, it has always been oppressive. It tends to put all the responsibility for my relationship with God on my shoulders. If I am committed, then I am consistent, regular, disciplined, strong-willed. Hey, this doesn't sound like Christianity! It sounds like a diet!"

So what does Mike Yaconelli think is a better word? "In my new dictionary I discovered the word hunger, and my soul began to tingle. Faith wasn't so much a discipline as it was a hunger. I had been hungry for God from the very beginning."

That's where life begins, in the land on beyond perfection.

WE GO BEYOND GOODNESS TO GRACE

The world on beyond perfection is where we go beyond just saying yes to really understanding the meaning of the word no, and it's a place where we go beyond the enticing pull of legalism to genuine liberty in our relationship with God.

I might sum it up like this: In the land on beyond perfection, we go beyond goodness to grace. To be a moral person usually means to be a good person. But life needs more from us than mere goodness.

Thomas Long tells about the process of examining seminary students for ordination in a Presbyterian church in North Carolina. The students must pass an intense examination out in the church somewhere. The ministers in the area get to grill a student on any point of theology for as long as they wish, and sometimes the questioning lasts a long time.

Thomas Long says that one of his clergy colleagues who has served the same congregation for more than thirty years sits in silence throughout these ordeals. He never says a word, never asks a question, never demands a clarification, until the very end.

Then, just when the examination seems to have run its course, the questioners are getting tired, and the seminary graduate starts to think the ordeal is over, this gentleman stands. "Look out there," he says. He points to a large window at the side of their meeting hall. "Tell me when you see someone walking out there."

So the candidate sits there, neck craned, and looks for a while. "I see someone," he says.

"Do you know the person?" asks Long's friend.

"No, I don't."

Says the elderly gentleman, "Describe that person to me, theologically."

This sage of North Carolina claims that one of two answers is always given. When you sift through all the academic lingo and verbal padding, some seminary graduates say something like this: "There goes a sinner who's on his way to hell unless he repents and gives his life over to Christ."

The other answer goes something like this: "There goes a person who is a child of God. God loves that person so very much, and the best thing that can happen to him is to find out how good it is to love God in return."

"They're both right," says the elderly man behind the strange question. "That's what the scriptures and the church have always said. Still, as I've watched these fellows come and go over the years, the ones who answer my question the second way make better pastors. Mark my words!"

Do you believe it? If you do, then you probably have already peeked into the world of Jesus' wisdom, the world on beyond perfection. For when the roll is called up yonder, the grades on the report cards that make it won't be *A* for excellent, or *B* for good, or even *C* for nice try.

The only grade that will make it will be *G* for grace.

"You have heard that it was said to the people long ago, 'Do not murder, and anyone who murders will be subject to judgment.' But I tell you that anyone who is angry with his brother will be subject to judgment. Again, anyone who says to his brother, 'Raca,' is answerable to the Sanhedrin. But anyone who says, 'You fool!' will be in danger of the fire of hell.

"Therefore, if you are offering your gift at the altar and there remember that your brother has something against you, leave your gift there in front of the altar. First go and be reconciled to your brother; then come and offer your gift.

"Settle matters quickly with your adversary who is taking you to court. Do it while you are still with him on the way, or he may hand you over to the judge, and the judge may hand you over to the officer, and you may be thrown into prison. I tell you the truth, you will not get out until you have paid the last penny."

—Matthew 5:21–26

4
THE WIT TO WIN

Building Bridges Instead of Walls

THE FOLLOWING IS a great poem by Edwin Markham:

> He drew a circle that shut me out—
> Heretic, rebel, a thing to flout.
> But love and I had the wit to win:
> We drew a circle that took him in!

It's beautiful, isn't it? In the face of attitudes that would kill, "love and I had the wit to win: we drew a circle that took him in."

The heart of what Jesus tells us in Matthew 5:21–26 is essentially that love reaches out.

Sometimes we point to people like Adolf Hitler, shake our heads, and call him a murderer. And we should. There's no excuse in the world for what he did. He's a murderer, and we all know it.

But Jesus forces us to take one step further. He talks to us about circles of death and circles of life, circles that shut people out of our lives, and circles that bring them in. The act of murder, Jesus says, is merely an attitude that's come full circle.

At the end of World War II, the great German theologian Reinhold Niebuhr said, "We must finally be reconciled with our foe, lest we both perish in the vicious circle of hatred." That's the kind of thing Jesus tells us here.

We could spend a lot of time talking about killing and murder and abortion, but if we stop there, we'll miss the essential thing that Jesus talks about. You see, the folks he spoke to had a high sense of morality. They couldn't tolerate murderers in their communities. They knew very well what the sixth commandment of God said: You shall not kill! They also knew the penalties against murderers in the laws of Moses.

But righteous indignation against people like Charles Manson and Jeffrey Dahmer is never enough. The murderer is not just a strange and twisted figure out there. The murderer also lives in each of us.

Of course, death isn't always murder, nor is it always painful. I remember the Friday evening when one of my grandmothers died in Minnesota. She was almost ninety-three years old. My Dad called and said that it was a great thing for her to go home to be with the Lord. Death was a welcome doorway into eternity. She once told me that one of her favorite verses in the Bible was in the final chapter of the Song of Songs. The whole book is about love and is summed up in chapter 6 this way: "Love is stronger than death!"

Question for us, as we listen to Rabbi Jesus, include: How is love stronger than death? What is it that we win when we draw circles of love?

Three things, answers Jesus.

I WIN A BROTHER

The first of the three is found in verses 21–22. We win a brother. We win a friend.

In one community where I lived, there were two brothers who farmed together. One was a bachelor and the other was married. For years they had worked together, one running the dairy, one taking care of the land. Things went along just fine. Then the bachelor brother got married to a beautiful woman. Shortly after that a baby came along.

That led the brothers to start thinking about the future. Maybe it was time for them to split the operation so that each family could have its own share. That's when the trouble began. They divided the land and the machinery, and then each took half of the cows. But after a couple of years, one herd began to produce more milk than the other.

One of the wives felt cheated. The other brother must have gotten the better cows. So she complained. It didn't take long before her husband went to his brother in a huff. Obviously his brother had worked it out somehow so that he got the best producing cows. He'd cheated his own brother!

That's when the fights began. They started calling each other names, like the ones Jesus talks about here: "Fool!" "Idiot!" "Liar!"

They used to sit next to each other in church, but they began choosing opposite doors and opposite sides. One of the couples called an elder and myself, as pastor, to come over. "Tell them they're doing wrong," they said. "Force them to give us a better deal!"

Then one wife stopped coming to church. And when her husband's term as deacon was finished, he left the church, too. They never came back.

Who won? Nobody.

Who lost? Everybody. The brothers each lost a brother. The children lost respect for their parents. The church lost members, and Christ lost his people. They started it all by saying, "You fool!" And in the end, only the fires of hell were the richer.

Maybe that's an extreme case. Still, we know that the same thing plays in every human heart. We draw circles around ourselves constantly: the circle of pride, the circle of jealousy, the circle of bitterness.

There are fourteen words in the Bible that have the meaning "to kill someone intentionally." Several of them speak of thoughts of the mind and attitudes of the heart rather than acts of the hand. One word means "to devalue" another person until that person has no worth. A woman remembers something that happened years ago. Someone hurt a friend of hers. Later the man in question becomes her Shepherding Elder at church, but she won't let him visit. She won't even talk with him. She draws a circle, and he is on the outside. Because of it they both lose.

Another word used in the Bible means "to separate" myself from others. A man sits with a load of bitterness. Someone has done him wrong. He's never going to forget it and neither is anyone else who comes near him. The circle is drawn, and every year it gets tighter.

Who wins? No one.

So what if your name isn't Jeffrey Dahmer. Do you suppose that murder of the heart isn't a crime? Do you think you can get by with it, just because you've got a good reason for it, at least in your own mind? Only hell wins. You lose. I lose. We lose.

But when love reaches out past hurts, something astounding happens. A psychologist named Kinch described it this way, back in 1967. Five graduate students in psychology at one university, he said, created a rather bizarre experiment. They were part of the "in" crowd at the university. They moved in the right circles. They dressed the right way, had the right friends, and went to the right places.

They decided to focus their attention on one young woman who wasn't in that circle. She was an outsider, a nobody, a person who didn't count, at least to them. Normally they wouldn't even talk with her. Yet, for the duration of the experiment, these fellows agreed to treat her like she was one of their crowd, like she was a somebody. They decided to talk with her, to call her up, and to ask her out. They made an agreement that whenever they saw her, they would compliment her and show an interest in her.

After a little while, as they carried on this experiment, something strange began to happen. She became more likable. She became less foreign, less alien.

The first fellow's date with her was hardly bearable. He had to keep repeating to himself: "She's beautiful. She's beautiful. I've got to keep telling myself that she's beautiful." By the time the third fellow asked her out, however, she had become part of their circle of friends. It was kind of fun being with her. She wasn't so bad after all. And the fifth fellow never did get to date her because the fourth fellow in line asked her to be his wife.

Now, that may have been a cruel experiment at the beginning, and certainly not something to try again, but isn't it amazing what can happen when we redraw the circles of our lives?

He drew a circle that shut me out—
Heretic, rebel, a thing to flout.
But love and I had the wit to win:
We drew a circle that took him in!

What do I win in the circle of love? I win a sister. I win a brother. That's what Jesus says in verses 21–22.

I WIN A FATHER

In verses 23–24 Jesus tells of a second thing that we win in the circle of love, and that's a Father. Do you see the picture there? A person has come to the Temple to worship God. She brings her offering. She gives it to the priests who will burn it as a sacrifice. She knows that her prayers will be heard by God in heaven, just as the smoke of the offering drifts toward the skies.

Yet somehow, this time, it doesn't seem to work. Her religion is useless. Her prayers bounce back from the ceiling. Her songs sound empty and hollow, and God is silent.

Did you ever feel that? Did you ever feel like God was off on holidays, and things around you operated randomly, all meaningless?

A close friend to Elvis Presley remembers a time shortly before the singer's death. Elvis was in his music room, with the volume turned way up as one song played over and over: "How Great Thou Art."

The man asked Elvis, "How are you doing?"

Elvis answered with a single word: "Lonely."

Lonely. That's the picture Jesus paints, isn't it? When we've left things undone between ourselves and others, somehow we can't find God either.

A friend of mine came to see me because she couldn't get it together spiritually. She wanted to be a Christian. She wanted to love God. But something always seemed to trip her up, to foil her best attempts, to keep her from the delight she wanted to have.

One day her mother asked to see me. She told me a tale that made it all fit together. Years before, when my friend was in eleventh grade, she got pregnant. She talked with her parents about it, and it was a tense time in the household.

One morning, when the family got up, my friend was missing. She had sneaked out during the night and disappeared. Her parents were frantic. They called her boyfriend. He didn't have a clue where she was. He said they weren't even together anymore. They called her closest girlfriend. She was missing too.

The police didn't act on it right away. Two runaways. Nothing they could do. But then she came home. She and her friend had gone together to an abortion clinic. The thing was done.

Her mother related to me that sometimes in the night her daughter still hears her baby cry. Not the three she has with her wonderful husband, but the baby that slipped out of her body that night on the edge of a knife. She sits up in bed at night and she hears her baby cry, and she can't find God.

The great preacher William Holmes used to tell the story of a beggar who came to the door of a magnificent mansion and asked for a bit to eat. "Go around to the back," he was told. There the master of the house met him. The gentleman carried a plate of food. Since he was a Christian, he wanted to set a good example, so he told the beggar, before he ate, that first they must ask for God's blessing.

"Just repeat after me," he said. "'Our father.'"

"Your father," said the poor man.

"No, no!" said the master of the house. "Let's try it again: 'Our Father.'"

"Your Father," said the beggar again.

"No!" said the rich man. "Didn't you hear me? I said, 'Our Father!'"

"Well, sir," answered the other man, "I figured that if I said, 'Our Father,' that'd make you and me brothers, and I'm not sure the Lord would like it, you makin' your brother come beggin' at the back door for a scrap of bread."

That's true, isn't it? In fact, later in the New Testament, the apostle James writes, "Religion that God our Father accepts as pure and faultless is this: to look after the orphans and widows in their distress . . ." (James 1:27). He reminds us that in some way, when we draw a small circle around ourselves and keep others at a distance, we keep God away from us, too.

Jesus said essentially the same thing in one of his parables. He said that at the end of time, when we face the Father, he'll talk with us about the way we treated those around us in this life: the poor, the lonely, the outcast. The ones that are shut out from the "pleasant" circles of life. He'll look at us with loving eyes, and he'll tell us of the ways that we reached out to him. "Whatever you did to the least of these," he'll say, "you did to me as well!"

But some of us will blush and burn at that moment. We will remember these lines: "You drew a circle that shut me out— Heretic, rebel, a thing to flout." And the eyes of the Father will be sad. And then we'll know what we've missed in life. We'll have lost a lot of brothers and sisters. But we'll also have lost our Father in heaven.

"There are no ordinary people," says C. S. Lewis in one of his sermons. "Next to the Blessed Sacrament itself, your neighbor is the holiest object presented to your senses." When you win your neighbor by lengthening the circle of your love, you come closest to touching God himself.

I WIN MYSELF

There's a third thing that Jesus speaks about in verses 25–26. When you expand the circle of love, you win a brother, you win a father, and you win yourself as well. Jesus makes it clear: when you draw the circles of fear and hatred and bitterness around yourself, the one who gets hurt the most is you.

Ibn Saud was the first modern king of Saudi Arabia. He lived during the early half of the twentieth century, and people in the East still talk about his wisdom. One day a widow came to him in a rage. She wanted justice against the man who had killed her husband. The story was strange: her husband had been walking under a palm tree when the other man, up in the tree gathering dates, slipped and fell on him. Her husband eventually died from internal injuries received in that accident.

Ibn Saud checked the matter out and found it was true. He asked the widow, "What compensation will you take?"

He thought that she would want a pension in order to care for her family in the years ahead. But instead she asked that her husband's unintentional killer be put to death. She wanted the other man to die. She drew a circle that shut him out.

Ibn Saud knew that her family needed support, not revenge. So quietly and calmly, he tried to talk her out of it. But she was adamant. Her husband was dead, and his slayer must die, too. There was no way to get her off her singular track.

When he saw that his coaxing was useless, Ibn Saud tried one more thing. He agreed to the death penalty, but he decreed that it be carried out in a very specific way. The man who killed her husband, he said, would be bound and set under a palm tree. Then the widow herself must climb the tree and throw herself down on the man, killing him.

"But I might also die!" she protested.

"Yes," said the king, "but hasn't your thirst for revenge already destroyed your soul? Aren't you just as dead as you wish him to be?"

The widow relented. She let the man live, and she received back her own life.

In much the same way, Jesus says here that when you create an adversary, in the end, you will always be the loser. Frederick Buechner writes that anger is the most fun of the Seven Deadly Sins. Anger makes you feel like you're feasting on a banquet fit for a king: you lick your wounds; you smack your lips over grievances long past; you roll over your tongue the prospect of bitter confrontations l to come; you savor to the last morsel the pain you are given and the pain you give back.

There's only one problem. In the end, when the meal is over, you find that you've eaten yourself. You've consumed your own flesh, and you're the one who has died.

That's what Jesus is saying as well. If you don't settle matters with someone who has become your enemy, you yourself will die a slow death in the prison of your bitterness. The word resentment could be defined to re-feel, to feel again and again and again. Every time you feel it, the pain gets deeper, the agony grows, and the bitterness wraps itself tighter. Someone hurts you once, but then you keep hurting yourself again and again and again as you think about it, and remember it, and go over every detail in livid color.

There is a wise saying in the Hebrew Talmud: "A person who carries a grudge is like a man who accidentally cuts one hand with a knife, and then stabs his other hand because it slipped." Imagine a hunter skinning his game with his hunting knife. He holds the warm flesh with his left hand while he slits the skin with the knife in his right hand. But the knife slips and cuts deep into his left hand. Blood spurts and the hunter shouts in pain.

What is he likely to do? Will he clean the wound and bandage it? That would be wise. But imagine the hunter instead becomes angry with his right hand for causing the wound to his left. His left hand gropes for the fallen weapon and stabs his right hand, returning pain for pain, avenging the first cut with a deeper gash. If we were to watch this incident we would roll our eyes at such idiocy.

Yet, in some way, this is what Jesus is trying to tell us. If we carry a grudge against someone who offends us we are not seeking healing; instead we are replaying the hurt to bring greater pain. We are as foolish as the hunter, more maimed than if we had sought healing instead of revenge. If I react to hurt by paying someone back tit-for-tat, then, as with the hunter, two wounds bleed instead of one, and no healing can begin. I lose my brother, and I lose something inside myself that becomes monstrous against him. Only when Love and I have "the wit to win," when we draw "a circle that [takes] him in," do I gain something of myself back again.

Author Dale Galloway tells of a friend who had a very shy son named Chad. The other children didn't usually include Chad in their circle of friends. Every afternoon his mother saw the school bus stop and all the children pile off in groups, laughing, playing, and joking with each other. Chad would be the last to come down the steps, always alone.

One day in late January, Chad came home and said, "Know what, Mom? Valentine's Day is coming, and I want to make a card for every single person in my class!"

Chad's mother felt terrible. She thought Chad was setting himself up for a fall. He was going to make valentines for everyone else, but nobody would think of him. He would come home all disappointed and just pull back further in his shell.

Still Chad insisted. So they got paper and crayons and glue. Chad made thirty-one valentine cards. It took him three weeks. The day he took them to school, his mother cried. And when he came off the bus, alone as usual, no valentine cards from anyone else in his hands, she was ready for the worst.

But Chad's face was glowing as he marched through the door triumphantly. "I didn't forget anybody!" he said. "I gave them all one of my hearts!" (Dale Galloway, *Dream a New Dream* [Wheaton:Tyndale, 1975]).

That day Chad gained something more than friends. He gained himself. He won a sense of dignity and worth.

That's how Jesus wants us to live. Circles of hatred erased by circles of love. Circles of bitterness blurred by circles of caring. Circles of death that give way to circles of life.

Isn't that what God has done for us? "While we were still sinners," says the apostle Paul, "Christ died for us!" (Romans 5:8). When we had drawn God out of our circles, his love drew us in. When we counted him as our enemy, he called to us as his friends. When we hardened the walls of our hearts against him, he softened us with his love.

After all, couldn't that poem be the conversation of heaven, the talk between the Father and the Son about you and me?

> He drew a circle that shut me out—
> Heretic, rebel, a thing to flout.
> But Love and I had the wit to win:
> We drew a circle that took him in!

Love is stronger than Death. The day Jesus drew a circle of love that took us in is the day Death died. Now we are free to live and draw circles like our Savior.

"You have heard that it was said, 'Do not commit adultery.' But I tell you that anyone who looks at a woman lustfully has already committed adultery with her in his heart. If your right eye causes you to sin, gouge it out and throw it away. It is better for you to lose one part of your body than for your whole body to be thrown into hell. And if your right hand causes you to sin, cut it off and throw it away. It is better for you to lose one part of your body than for your whole body to go into hell.

"It has been said, 'Anyone who divorces his wife must give her a certificate of divorce.' But I tell you that anyone who divorces his wife, except for marital unfaithfulness, causes her to become an adulteress, and anyone who marries the divorced woman commits adultery. "

—*Matthew 5:27–32*

5
BEAUTIFUL MUSIC ON THE HUMAN STEREO

Bringing Sex Back into the Church, Where It Belongs

I HAD LUNCH one day with a pastor of a neighboring congregation who wanted to welcome me to the community. We were old friends and had a great time reminiscing and catching up. That night, when we were talking together as a family about the things we'd done during the day, my wife Brenda asked me where we had crossed paths before.

"Well," I said, "his sister was my first girlfriend."

Of course, *that* got the attention of a few ears. "Daddy?" asked one of our daughters, "did you think a lot about girls when you were a teenager?" I had to admit that I did.

There was no stopping this thing now. "Mommy?" came the next question, "did *you* think a lot about boys when you were a teenager?" I looked at Brenda, eager to hear the answer, too.

"Yes," said Brenda, "I did."

They were on a roll now. "Mommy and Daddy, why do teenagers like each other so much?"

What do you say?

I remember what Chuck Swindoll said one time. He was speaking at a conference, and one morning a woman handed him a note. In it she told him that she had gotten married at the age of thirty-one. She said that she hadn't been worried too much about being single until then, although she did have a rather peculiar practice. Every night, before she went to sleep, she hung a pair of men's pants on the headboard of her bed. Then she knelt next to her bed, held onto the trousers with one hand, and prayed this prayer:

Father in heaven, hear my prayer,
And grant it if you can;
I hung a pair of trousers here—
Please fill them with a man!

That's a good story, but something happened to Chuck Swindoll that makes it even better. He shared this story with his congregation the following Sunday morning. The crowds, of course, roared with delight. Chuck did see one young man who didn't smile. In fact, he seemed a bit preoccupied.

The young man's mother wasn't in church with the family that morning, having stayed at home to take care of a sick daughter. But a couple of weeks later, the mother slipped a note to Chuck after worship. It read, "Dear Chuck, I am wondering if I should be worried about something with our son. For the last two weeks I have noticed that before he turns out the light at night he hangs a woman's bikini over the foot of his bed. . . . Should I be concerned about this?"

Why do boys and girls like each other so much? What should we say? Certainly, when Jesus reflects on marriage in the Sermon on the Mount, he has some things in mind about human sexual relations.

HUMAN SEXUALITY IS THE BEST THING THAT EVER HAPPENED TO US

First, the Bible indicates that our sexuality is the best thing that ever happened to us. In the story of creation, God fashions Adam to roam his beautiful new world. God brings all of the animals to him to play with, but they're not enough. He's alone in a crowd, so God creates Eve to be with Adam, someone like him in every way and yet so different.

In that act God declares that loneliness is bad—so bad that it doesn't belong in a world he declared "very good." The way to get around loneliness is to find a relationship that matters with a person who matters. God intended for that to happen with two genders.

Hugh Hefner is onto something, you know. He turned sex into a multi-billion dollar business with his *Playboy* magazine and his Playboy clubs. During a recent interview, when a reporter asked why he was so fixated on sex, Hefner said, "Sex is a function of the body. A drive which man shares with animals, like eating, drinking, and sleeping. It's a physical demand that must be satisfied. If you don't satisfy it, you will have all sorts of neurosis and repression psychosis. Sex is here to stay. Let's forget the prudery that makes us hide from it. Throw away those inhibitions, find a girl who's like-minded, and let yourself go!"

In many respects, I think Hefner is right. God made us males and females, and he wanted us to enjoy one another in just that way.

Stan Wiersma, who taught at Calvin College until his death some years ago, wrote a collection of eighteen poems, one for each of his first eighteen years of life. He collected them in a book called *Purpaleanie* (Orange City, Iowa:Middleburg Press, 1978). In "Seventeen," he recalls his own sex education on the farm, and writes to his father, who is the "you":

Mother worried
that my sex education
was not complete, not knowing
you had undertaken it when I was one.

Mother called a family council
before I went to college.
Mother led off:

"Love is never sin.
  Lust is always sin.
Love is giving.
  Lust is taking.

Love always lasts.
    Lust never lasts.
Love is expressing yourself.
    Lust is gratifying yourself."

And you, Dad,
suddenly agitated:
"This uncivilized English
language, with two words for the same thing,
only one is good and the other bad! In Dutch
lust means like wanting food when you're hungry!
Sure, it's getting,
    it never lasts,
        and it's self-gratifying,
but it's not sin to enjoy food when you're hungry!"

Then you fell silent.
When you spoke again
you were calmer.

"When you get married, Sietze,
I hope it's for love,
but I hope it's for lust too."

Don't imagine that Adam was a prude. Don't think that Eve was shy about being a woman. Don't pretend that Jesus didn't understand what it was like to be male. After all, he's one of the three persons of the holy Trinity of God who said together, at the beginning of time, "Let's make humankind in *our* image, . . . male *and* female."

That doesn't mean that the persons of the holy Trinity of God are male and female; rather, it reminds us that the persons of the Trinity had such a wonderful relationship together that they wanted others to share whatever was good about it. When they scattered the stars and the planets across the universe, and when they condensed the moisture of the earth into seas and clouds, and when they planned together the human form, they must have said to one another: "We've got to give these humans the delightful relationship we share with each other." The best way they could figure to make that happen was to fix some of us up as females and to fix others of us up as males.

God himself declares, at the beginning of time, that the best thing that's ever happened to us is our human sexuality.

THE PURPOSE OF OUR HUMAN SEXUALITY IS TO FIND DEEPER IDENTITY

But Jesus isn't just talking about human sexuality in these verses. He also addresses the major threats to marriage: adultery and divorce. In what Jesus says, he affirms the sanctity of marriage. He shouts in a large voice that marriage is holy. Jesus declares that there is something very special about marriage, and that *no one* ought to tamper with.

Why is marriage such a sacred thing? It has to do, in part, with our search for self. Notice that when Jesus speaks of someone committing adultery, he gives the impression that that person doesn't really comprehend the outcome of his or her actions. The same is true with the person who divorces. Divorce means somebody wasn't in touch with the self. The person divorcing doesn't understand what this action means for all the parties involved.

We come into this world as *unfinished* creatures; works in progress. Little babies are fully human, but no one would say that they are fully developed. They have a lifetime of potential growth and development ahead of them. Intellectually, they will need teachers to pour waters of learning into the sponges of their minds. Volitionally, they will need parental discipline to shape and mold and give contour to the persons they are becoming. Socially, they will respond to friends and communities, until they find a way to be themselves in relation with others.

Still, chances are that they won't truly find themselves in a very personal way without help from someone of the opposite sex. Says A. E. Houseman:

> When I was in love with you
> Then I was clean and brave!
> And miles around the wonder grew
> How well I did behave!

He's saying that something of himself came alive *only* when he found himself in relationship with another.

I remember how it was to fall in love for the first time. No one understood me like she did. Definitely not any of my other friends. Certainly not my parents. *I* didn't even understand myself as much as she understood me. One of the most fascinating parts of our courtship was our conversations together. We could talk about *everything.* She helped me to understand who I was just because she was there for me.

Renowned psychiatrist Rollo May says in his book *Love and Will* (New York: Delta, 1969) that loving a person of the opposite sex and finding intimacy with that person has five deepening dimensions to it. Some of them are relevant to us here.

First, he says, there's a tenderness that happens to us which softens our hard walls of self, and which penetrates the mighty defenses we use to protect our individuality. Remember the old song about love that Jimmy Dean made popular:

> Six foot six he stood on the ground,
> Weighed two hundred and thirty-five pounds!
> Yet I saw that giant of a man brought down to his knees by love!

So it is with us. Our individuality makes us scramble for a personal identity. At the same time, our sinfulness makes us fight for our distinction from everyone else. But something about love burrows past our rocks and walls and pride and opens us to the wonder that there might be in intimacy with that special person. The poet A. D. Hope puts it this way:

> Here I come home: in this expected country
> They know my name and speak it with delight.

I am the dream and you my gates of entry.
The means by which I waken into the light.

I was asleep, unaware of who I was, until you spoke my name, until you called me awake, until you brought me home to myself for the first time. This is the tenderness of love that works its magic on our crusty selves.

Second, says Rollo May, there's the affirmation of myself in a relationship of love. Social scientists talk to us about the culture of space. We each draw a circle around us wherever we go, whatever we do. In North America that circle is about three-to-four feet wide. It extends from the center of the body approximately eighteen inches to two feet in every direction. It's the space we claim for ourself, the space we "own" as we move in this physical realm.

The circle is our personal space, and we won't easily let someone enter it. Notice it next time you are in a crowd. Most people will keep others about eighteen inches to two feet from the centers of themselves. And if someone should be so bold as to invade our space, what do we do? A nice person will lean slightly away from the other person, or perhaps take a step back. A child or rude adult will give the other person a good push back into his or her own space.

In different societies the size of the circle changes. In Nigeria, where we served as missionaries, the circle was much smaller—only about two feet wide. But every culture has personal space that is guarded with great tenacity.

We guard our space because we're afraid someone else might dominate our identity. We're afraid another person will overpower who we are. We're afraid that we'll lose our sense of self if someone else comes too near.

But what happens to us when we fall in love? Suddenly we can't get close enough to our beloved. It has been said that the scientific term for holding hands is "premarital interdigitation." It's part of that closeness we allow to only someone special. "Here," we say, "you can come into my space. That's right. Come on in. Here, let me hold the door for you. Sure, come right on in."

The only reason we can do that is because in love we know the other person affirms us, rather than seeking to annihilate us. That's the second thing love means to us: it affirms who we are.

The *third* dimension of love, says Rollo May, is the creative element. There's something about love which convinces us that together we're more than the combination of our individual selves. I give to you. You give to me. And somehow in the giving a greater identity is formed.

A friend of mine during our college years found this to be true. He was part of a group that included about fifteen or so companions, two-thirds of which were female. They treated one another as sisters and brothers, never actually dating within the group. One young woman was a particularly close confidant to my friend. They took long walks together, sharing everything.

Then one day someone began courting my friend's female companion. Suddenly his conversations about her changed. They still walked and talked and sat and went for coffee together or with others of the group. But now my friend became excited about her in a way that he hadn't before. It wasn't that he wanted to date her, although I think some fires of jealousy were kindled at times. Mostly, though, it was that energy created through her blossoming relationship with another fellow that brought out dreams and goals and insights and zest for living that astounded him. He thought he knew her so well, but then she suddenly began to glow even brighter. Because of love, her qualities of personhood stretched in wonderful new ways.

God, of course, beautifully confirms the creative energy of lovers through the blessing of children. In a real sense, children are the two selves of the parents that come together to form a greater new self.

The *fourth* dimension of love is closely tied to the third. It's the giving dimension. Love teaches us the truth of Jesus' statement, "It is more blessed to give than to receive." Giving is the beginning of receiving where love is concerned. Why do lovers give each other gifts? Is it to buy back something in return? You know it's not. Lovers give because it is the meaning of love itself.

Read C. S. Lewis on love sometime. In *The Four Loves*, he explores the four Greek words meaning love which were available in Jesus' day.

There's *storge,* which means kind thoughts and affection. It's the type of love children have for pets. There's *philia,* which is the tenderness of friendship. *Eros* always has a physical dimension to it.

And then, says Lewis, there was also a little-used term: *agape.* Nobody was using it much anymore, but somebody forgot to take it out of the dictionary. Along came Jesus and the church, and they suddenly shouted it everywhere.

Agape means a love which reaches beyond the warm fuzzies of itself and seeks to bring life and joy and delight and meaning to another person. *Agape* is the Bible's word of love. "We love," says John, "because God first loved us." The word John uses is *agape.* The giving love. The love that reaches beyond itself to touch another life with beauty. When the other dimensions of love are there, according to Rollo May, the fifth and final dimension happens. It's the dimension of shared consciousness.

Poet John Betjeman remembers a sacred moment in a tiny tea shop in Bath, England. He sat at his table and watched an elderly couple enter. They took a booth nearby and ordered a pot of tea and some crumpets. Then he recorded their conversation in his own words:

> "Let us not speak, for the love we bear one another—
> Let us hold hands and look."
> She, such a very ordinary little woman;
> He, such a thumping crook;
> But both, for a moment, little lower than the angels
> In the tea shop's ingle-nook.

This is a picture of the intimacy of love when identities begin to fuse. It's what the Apostle Paul meant when he said, "Have this mind in you which was also in Christ Jesus . . ." For the deepest dimension of love is to share, beyond the physical realities, the consciousness of the other.

God made us males and females because we would only be able to plumb the depths of ourselves more fully when we found ourselves in relation with someone of the opposite sex. We call it culture. When you start learning the culture of the other gender, and the language that expresses it, you begin to better understand your own language.

So it is with our human sexuality. Many have noted that the language of males seems to be of one kind, while the language of females is another. In some sense males can never really understand their own language, with all its hidden culture and biases, until they learn something of the female lingo. Similarly, females can never really understand their own language until they learn something of the male lingo.

In fact, the more each of us has the ability to learn of the other language, the more we begin to understand our own native speech. We begin to understand the culture of our own hearts as we find our deeper identity through relationships across the gender divide.

OUR GREATEST NEED IN FINDING THAT IDENTITY IS LOVE AND SAFETY

Our greatest need in finding that identity is love and safety. This is why Jesus says pointed things about adultery and divorce. No one in this world knows me better than my wife, and no one in this world has helped me to know myself better than Brenda has. The reason we have gained access to each other has to do with safety. I can share bits and pieces of myself with many people. I can share moments and thoughts with close friends. But with Brenda, I'm learning to share everything that I am in all five dimensions of love.

How does a couple develop that intimacy? Like this: Brenda has created a safe place for me. Our marriage is a sanctuary of safety where we can express and explore those dimensions of love. If I am to enter her space, if I am to gain access to a place that allows me to find my truest self, if I am to learn the female language in order to understand my own native tongue, then I have to know that she will not violate me. She will not ridicule or demean me, she will not destroy me, she will not use me and toss me aside, and she will not abuse our intimacy.

If I am to find myself, I need to know that she wants me to find myself, and that she wants to find me as well—not to abuse, but to cherish.

This is where we fulfill our greatest sexual need: within the sanctity of marriage. Dr. Nancy Moore Clatworthy, a renowned sociologist, spent ten years researching people who lived together without being married. When she began her research, she was convinced that living together was a good thing, perhaps even a better thing than the stuffiness of marriage.

Yet she wanted to prove it in a scientific way. For that reason, she interviewed hundreds of couples who were living together, observing the development of people as their lives unfolded.

Amazingly, in spite of her own wishes, she found that living together without marriage is one of the worst things for the human person because the context of safety is gone. People who move in together view the relationship as non-committed sharing, so they can never fully give themselves to the other person in the relationship. Why should I give myself to you if tomorrow you can walk right out of here? Why should I trust you with my intimate self if I don't know whether you'll protect me when you find me?

Dr. Clatworthy now vehemently opposes co-habitation outside of marriage. She says that our human sexuality *demands* the safety of marriage in order for us to become the persons we can be, the persons we are supposed to be.

Other studies confirm Dr. Clatworthy's research. The results of a scientific survey were published recently in Canada under this title: "A Hazard Model Analysis of the Covariates of Marriage Dissolution in Canada." It said that those who choose to live with someone of the opposite sex before marriage were twice as likely to have the relationship end in divorce as those who didn't cohabit first. Why? Because if this is a trial relationship, I will never be able to believe that you won't walk out on me. The possibility of finding the safety to be my truest self is gone.

Studies in Sweden and here in the U. S. say the same thing. If you want your marriage to fail, the best thing you can do is live with the other person before getting married. You'll never be able to fully trust anyone again. More than that, you'll have denied yourself one of the best opportunities for finding yourself.

So it is with adultery. The safety is gone. You slash away the curtain that hides our special room, and you leave me standing naked in someone else's bedroom.

Similarly, divorce rips a person apart. If the highest of the five dimensions of love is joining my identity with yours, how can I find myself again after you hack with your knife between us? Divorce rips something irreplaceable out of me. It tears a gaping hole in our sacred safe space. I'm left exposed, and incomplete. I'm left with less than I had before I met you, because you take part of me away with yourself.

This is why Jesus had such strong words about adultery. This is why Jesus had such strong words about divorce, because they are worse than death. They kill the spirit without ending the life of the body.

Listen to Oliver Stone, the creative power behind a number of major movies such as *Born on the Fourth of July* and *JFK*. During a newspaper interview, Stone explained that both he and his friend had been divorced recently. Yet, while Stone's friend seemed comfortable with his new circumstances, Oliver Stone himself was wasted. "I was in a fairly sad mood," said Stone, "because of my own divorce problems, and I was thinking, 'Look at him! He's got his life together. He's made it. Something's wrong with me.'"

But then came news of his friend's arrest for the murder of his former wife and her lover. This is what Oliver Stone then said of his friend: "He was too nice all the time. So one night he blows. Anybody who's been through divorce will tell you that at one point they've thought of murder. The line between thinking murder and doing murder isn't that major!" (Quoted in *USA Today*, August 2, 1994, page 2D.)

Neither, it would seem, is the line between divorce and the death it can cause inside a person.

SEXUAL PERVERSIONS AND ADULTERY ARE SERIOUS CRIMES

Sexual perversions are such serious crimes: domestic violence, incest, and rape. Each of them cuts at the heart of our human identity. Each of them violates the safe space we need in order to find ourselves. Each of them robs us of something essential to our characters.

The first question we ask when a child is born is this: "Is it a boy or a girl?" Our sexuality is as basic as our human existence, and when someone steals away from us something of that sexual identity, our very lives are demeaned!

That's why Jesus uses such strong language for anyone who presses that edge: "Cut your eye out! Saw off your hand!" If you take someone's car, you can pay them back. But if you violate someone's sexuality, you destroy something of their very souls. You can never undo the damage.

I hope the message is clear. The best that can happen to you, happens to you as a sexual person. And the worst that can happen to you, happens to you as a sexual person. God meant for you to enjoy your sexuality to the fullest. In fact, only in sexual relationship with another person will you begin to find your truest self. That's why Jesus cautions us to deal wisely with each other in sexual relations, because the greatest violence that can happen to someone happens when we violate him or her sexually. Don't let it happen!

We as males and females have grown embattled against one another in our society. Christ can break down the barriers between us. Where we are presently engaged in activities that would harm others or ourselves sexually, Christ can help us overcome the worst evil in our souls. Where we have been horribly wronged by others and where we have horribly wronged others, Christ can lead us through the hurting and healing steps of forgiveness. Where our marriages have ended in divorce, Christ can give us a second chance to find sexual meaning and intimacy and identity. Where marriage is not a possibility for us, Christ can make our lives full and complete in ways that transcend even our sexuality.

The human race is like a radio. It can make a lot of noise, and it can produce a lot of music, but the best sounds come in stereo—female and male. And the best music happens when the system is tuned to the frequency God designed for it.

"Again, you have heard that it was said to the people long ago, 'Do not break your oath, but keep the oaths you have made to the Lord.' But I tell you, Do not swear at all: either by heaven, for it is God's throne; or by the earth, for it is his footstool; or by Jerusalem, for it is the city of the Great King. And do not swear by your head, for you cannot make even one hair white or black. Simply let your 'Yes' be 'Yes,' and your 'No,' 'No'; anything beyond this comes from the evil one."

—*Matthew 5:33–37*

6
STRAIGHT TALK

Checking the Sound of Our Heart Monitor

Mark Twain tells of a hot summer afternoon in his boyhood when the horizon shimmered. It made him thirsty just looking at it. As Twain walked down a street, he spied a cart piled high with watermelons. He loved watermelons.

He glanced around, strolled by, and lifted one from the top. Quick as a flash he disappeared down an alley. "[I] sank my teeth into the melon," he says. "[But] no sooner had I done so . . . than a strange feeling came over me. Without a moment's hesitation, I made my decision. I walked back to the cart, replaced the melon . . . and took a ripe one!"

Isn't that like us? It would be a rare person among us whose life has been without moments of deceit, deception, and dishonesty. Actually, that's exactly why Jesus says what he does in Matthew 5:33–37. He doesn't have a problem with oaths as such. In fact, he quotes a verse from Leviticus where God himself *tells* people to *take* oaths and to *keep* them. But he has a problem with what that has begun to mean about the way we are inside, and the way we treat each other.

Hopefully when we take an oath, it says that we are telling the truth. But, as Jesus indicates here, it can also say a whole lot more. When I must *swear* to you that I'm telling you the truth, it means that I ordinarily lie. It means that, under normal circumstance, you can't trust what I say.

Two people were walking through an English church yard, overcrowded with graves and tombstones. They read the inscriptions as they passed by. The first man read aloud, "'Here lies John Smith, a politician and an honest man.'"

"Good gracious!" said the second man. "Isn't it awful that they have to put two people in the same grave?"

Yet, when I take an oath, it can say that I'm really two people. Normally you can't trust me. Usually I don't tell you the truth. Unless I'm bound by this oath, you can't be sure that I'm honest. If that's what oaths are all about, Jesus has no use for them. Says A. M. Hunter, "Oaths arise because men are so often liars." That's what breaks Jesus' heart here. Says Dr. Johnson, "It requires no extraordinary talents to lie and deceive." That's the tragedy of our human situation.

A second thing that an oath says is that there are different degrees of truth. Jesus says that the people in his day swore to telling the truth in a variety of different ways. Sometimes they might say, "As sure as my hair is black, I'm telling you the truth!"

But how sure was that? Maybe you dyed your hair. Maybe it wasn't really your hair at all. That was okay when you were telling a fish story: "You should have seen the one that got away! It was thi-i-i-i-i-i-s big!" But if you really wanted to get them to believe you, you might say, "By the Temple in Jerusalem . . ." or "As sure as God is in his heaven . . ." Then you were honest, and they knew it. If you took that oath, they could see you were telling the truth.

Unfortunately this means that there are different levels of truth. There is ordinary truth, which probably is a bit of a lie. Then there's "courtroom" truth, which is probably more honest. Finally there is "religious" truth, which is supposed to be the most honest of all.

That's what upsets Jesus so much about oaths. We live in a society of lies, and we're proud of ourselves when we tell a half-truth. What a world we live in!

Straight talk, says Jesus. That's what we need. "Let your 'Yes' be 'Yes,' and your 'No,' 'No'; anything beyond this comes from the evil one."

STRAIGHT TALK MEANS FREEDOM

Straight talk means, first of all, freedom. When I've learned straight talk in my life, I've finally learned what it means to be free.

One person has said that when Judas betrayed Jesus for thirty pieces of silver, he didn't sell Jesus; he sold himself. He sold whatever there was inside of him that was good and clean and honest and godly. That was why he committed suicide later; though he had done something terrible and tragic, it was never beyond the scope of God's forgiving love. Peter betrayed Jesus too, and he didn't kill himself. In fact, Jesus helped him to find forgiveness and a new place in God's service.

But when Judas chose to do what he did, he sold himself. He took whatever there might have been inside of honesty and integrity and the character of God, and he sold it. He let it go, and later, when he looked inside, there was nothing to find.

Straight talk is the kind of integrity that sets us free to be our true selves, the selves God made us to be. We weren't born to lie. The Bible says that we were made in the image of God. When the psalmist talks about God he says: "Your word is Truth" (Psalm 119:160). When the apostle John talks about God, he says, "God is light . . . " and his ways are truth (1 John 1). And when Jesus tells us about our relationship with God, he says, "'Then you will know the truth, and the truth will set you free" (John 8:32).

A couple of centuries ago, Frederick the Great of Prussia arranged for an inspection tour of the Berlin prison. As he walked through the dungeons, all the inmates stretched their arms toward him and fell at his feet begging, "Your Majesty! Your Majesty! I'm an innocent man! I was sent here by my enemies! Speak the word! Free me from this dungeon!"

Every prisoner had the same tale. Every convict claimed to be truly a good man. Every inmate begged to be freed. Except for one man. He stood off in the corner by himself: no cries about injustice, no demands for freedom.

Frederick called out to him, "You there! Why are you here?"

"Armed robbery, your Majesty."

Asked Frederick, "Are you guilty?"

"Yes, your Majesty. I entirely deserve my punishment."

Frederick summoned the prison warden and ordered, "Release this guilty wretch at once! I will not have him kept in this prison where he will corrupt all the fine, innocent people who occupy it!"

That's a bit of the picture of what God has done for us. In a world of lies, in a society of advertising hype, in a community of half-truths, he shows us ourselves, what we're really like inside. Then, when we have nowhere to turn, he points to the truth of the Cross, and he sets us free. If there is any straight talk in our lives, it's a reflection of his straight talk to us.

A woman once came to me for counseling. We spent nearly two years talking about what was going on, what she felt, and what she needed. She was living a lie, and she didn't even know it. It had twisted her around in so many ways that she couldn't even say what the problem was. But finally God's straight talk got through to her, wrapped itself around her hurting heart, and took the kinks out of her troubled dreams.

She talks differently today. Her yes means yes, and she knows why. She no longer has to hide behind masks and clever tales and false fronts. She doesn't have to lie to God anymore, and she doesn't have to lie to herself. The doors of her prison swung open. She found God. She found herself. She's free, and the way she talks shows it.

STRAIGHT TALK MEANS DEPTH OF CHARACTER

The second thing straight talk means in our lives is depth of character.

I remember a book that one of my teachers read to our class when I was in elementary school. It moved me powerfully at the time, and I cried the day she finished it. The book was Marjorie Kinnan Rawlings' novel *The Yearling*. It's the story of a young boy in a backwoods county learning the lessons of life and becoming a man.

At one point in the story Penny Baxter, the boy's father, sets out to get rid of his no-good hunting dog. He knows that people usually talk a lot about their dogs. They stretch the truth a bit, just for excitement. In fact, the more you bragged about your dog, the more people knew you were lying.

So Penny Baxter takes his dog over to Lenn Forrester's place. Lenn asks him about his dog. "He ain't wuth a good twist o' t'bacy," says Penny. "Sorriest bear dog I ever follered!"

Lenn gets to thinking. He's never heard a man run down a dog like that before, and he decides that Penny is just trying to keep him from stealing it. So the next day Lenn brings over a fine shotgun. "Don't argue with me!" he says. "When I want a dog, I want a dog!" The deal is made.

Later, Penny Baxter's conscience begins to burn. "You told the truth, Pa!" his son says. But Penny knows different. "Yes," he said, "my words were straight, but my intention was as crooked as the Ocklawaha River."

That's what Jesus means here. People who tell the truth, even when they take an oath to tell it, aren't always being honest. There is more to truth-telling than just repeating the facts. Truth has depth of character, consistency of soul.

In *Scintilae Juris*, a law textbook written by a Justice of the British courts and published in 1889, the author makes this observation: "Much truth is spoken, that more may be concealed." Isn't that so often what takes place?

So, what if you tell the truth, but your heart wishes a lie? What if you give all the facts, but make it sound like something it isn't? You're a shallow person. There's no depth to you. There's no substance to your character. You're all show, all blow, all crow.

Martin Niemöller commanded a German submarine during World War I and earned respect as a patriot and a hero. Children looked up to him. Parents told their young to be like him. He was a man of integrity and honor. He went on to become a minister of the Gospel and took a pastorate on the outskirts of Berlin. Still, the depth of the straight talk of God that he preached every Sunday didn't come home to him until Hitler made him a prisoner at Dachau death camp.

When he was released, he told what he had learned about himself in those horrible days. "The Nazis came for the communists," he said, "and I didn't speak up because I wasn't a communist. Then they came for the Jews, and I didn't speak up because I wasn't a Jew. Then they came for the trade unionists, and I didn't speak up because I wasn't a trade unionist. Then they came for the Catholics, and I was a Protestant, so I didn't speak up. Then they came for me. By that time there was no one left to speak up for me."

Sad, isn't it? Sad but true. Said Robert Louis Stevenson, "The cruelest lies are often told in silence." And they're told by those who haven't grown deep in the truth of God.

There is an interesting picture of truth in the ceremonies of the Old Testament. We translate the Hebrew word *thom* to mean "integrity," and it carries with it the idea of wholeness, or completeness. The same word is also found in the Old Testament many times in its plural: *thummim.* In fact, the word *thummim* was the name of the stone on the High Priest's ceremonial clothing that was supposed to symbolize the speech of God.

The message to Israel was clear: when God spoke a word of instruction, it was good and right and just. When God declared his love, it was holy and pure and genuine. You could trust it. It had depth to it. It was complete. As F. M. Lehman states in the hymn, "The Love of God":

> Could we with ink the oceans fill,
> And were the skies of parchment made;
> Were every stalk on earth a quill,
> And every man a scribe by trade,
> To write the love of God above
> Would drain the oceans dry;
> Nor could the scroll contain the whole,
> Though stretched from sky to sky!

There is depth to God's character and his speech. And that's the quality you find in those who know God. There is depth to them. They have character that goes beyond the facts of the surface. They know the language of straight talk, the kind of thing that the song says, "Straight from the heart."

When Alexander Pope wrote, "An honest man is the noblest work of God," he was right. As Jesus indicates in Matthew 5:37, if you're not of the evil one, then you speak the straight talk of God. That's the most ennobling thing that can happen to you.

Much in our world is deceptive and dishonest: the rhetoric of government leaders can make one sick; the propaganda of advertising, with its slanted facts and figures and testimonials, creates cynics and skeptics. We can talk self-righteously about changing the world "out there," but instead we should work in ways that promote our own inner honesty and integrity and genuineness.

But it starts at home. It starts in hearts that have been to the Cross, where the Word of God, the straight talk of heaven, was raised up for all to see. It starts when women and men, girls and boys see the character of Jesus, the greatest straight talker of all time, and hear his words: "Take! Eat! Remember and believe!" Then they're joined with him in a new way of living, in a new way of talking, in a new depth of character.

Albert Schweitzer won the Nobel Prize in 1952 for the depth of his character. He was a brilliant musician and university professor, but he gave it all up to become a medical missionary to Africa. He was a man of great compassion, great love, and great integrity. He wasn't the most dynamic public speaker, but people couldn't miss the depth and warmth of his character. One evening he gave a public lecture and two theology students went to hear him. As they were leaving, one turned to the other and said, "He didn't really say that much, did he?"

An older man following them heard the remark and interrupted their conversation. "A man on a cross," he said, "doesn't have to say much."

That was true of Jesus. That was true of Albert Schweitzer. And that's true of all who learn the straight talk of God's love. It's not flowered up with all kinds of oaths and fancy words and testimonials. But it is true. And it is honest. And it carries the depth of character that comes to those who know God's love. It's the "Yes" that means yes, and the "No" that has his freedom to make important choices in life.

You don't need to swear if you talk straight.

"You have heard that it was said, 'Eye for eye, and tooth for tooth.' But I tell you, Do not resist an evil person. If someone strikes you on the right cheek, turn to him the other also. And if someone wants to sue you and take your tunic, let him have your cloak as well. If someone forces you to go one mile, go with him two miles. Give to the one who asks you, and do not turn away from the one who wants to borrow from you.

"You have heard that it was said, 'Love your neighbor and hate your enemy.' But I tell you: Love your enemies and pray for those who persecute you, that you may be sons of your Father in heaven. He causes his sun to rise on the evil and the good, and sends rain on the righteous and the unrighteous. If you love those who love you, what reward will you get? Are not even the tax collectors doing that? And if you greet only your brothers, what are you doing more than others? Do not even pagans do that? Be perfect, therefore, as your heavenly Father is perfect."

—Matthew 5:38–48

7
BUILDING A HEAVEN IN HELL'S DESPAIR

Taming the Volcano of Seething Bitterness

YEARS AGO I SERVED in Nigeria among the Tiv as a missionary-teacher at a training school for pastors. The Tiv are a beautiful people—strong, gracious, loyal. They are a clan of farmers planted by God on the shores of the Benue River in south central Nigeria. They are also a storytelling people, carrying their history and traditions with them in the tales they tell.

While we were living with the Tiv, a border clash erupted between the Tiv and the Udam. Ancient legends say that at one time, many generations ago, the Tiv were nomads, trekking through central Africa. In their wanderings, they had nearly come to ruin with starvation when they stumbled into Udam territory. The Udam people knew how to grow yams and taught the Tiv their secrets. Ever since that time, the Tiv settled along the Benue River and became farmers of yams.

But times changed, and the Tiv territory became Benue State in the new nation of Nigeria. The Udam region became known as Cross River State. But since the border between Benue State and Cross River State never exactly matched the tribal territorial bounds, the Udam and the Tiv became enemies, forever feuding at the arbitrary lines drawn in the sand and clay. Sometimes the Tiv would raid a border village of Udam and steal a treasure or claim a yam farm or take a life. Other times it would go the other way, and a raiding party from the Udam would slink in with knives and guns and leave a swath of bloodshed behind.

While we were teaching at RTCN in Nigeria, the border clashes erupted again. The story we heard was that a Tiv man married an Udam girl. When they became well-to-do on their farm, the girl's family grew jealous. They raided the farm one night, killed the Tiv man, burned his buildings and his crop, took his possessions, and stole away his wife, their sister.

Of course, the family of the Tiv man wouldn't let the crime go unpunished, so they retaliated in kind. Soon a war of vengeance was mushrooming around us. No session could begin at school until we talked about the latest developments in the fighting. One of my students in the Year Three class was gone for a week after his uncle was killed in the conflict and his family's village was burned. A student in Year One lost a grandfather. And one morning the caretaker of our compound showed up with a bloody bandage on his arm. He had narrowly escaped with his life after he met a roving band of Udam warriors.

Keep in mind, these are people of the twentieth century. They speak several languages, and carry out business and politics in English. They drive cars and operate heavy machinery. They listen to radios and watch television. And remember also that these are Christians. They were all trained in Christian schools. The people we were living with were students and faculty at a Christian seminary, a school that's preparing them to be pastors in Christian congregations.

Every Wednesday evening the staff had a Bible study. We were going through the Sermon on the Mount. Aheneka was leading one night. He was a quiet and thoughtful man, raised in a Christian home, trained in his theology at several North American seminaries, and ordained as a pastor in the Tiv church.

Joshua Yakubu, the Principal of the Seminary, sat next to him. Yakubu was a wizened gentleman, soft and humble. He exuded graciousness. At my right was Akpem, a scholar's scholar, ruled by reason as much as by common sense.

The hour for the session to begin passed, but this night there would be no Bible study because the talk was spitting in rage. "The Udam!

Curse their bloody souls! We shouldn't be sitting here tonight! We should be out there with guns and knives!"

I sat there, wobbling and teetering on a seething kettle of passion. I knew these people. They were Christians. They were kind. Any other day of the week I would entrust my life, my family, my welfare to any one of them. But tonight the fires of hell burned in their eyes. The room grew small with the heat of their blazing rage. If I mentioned the tempering grace of Christian forbearance, they might turn on me like a pack of dogs.

The Principal remembered a story of a previous tribal conflict. The Udam had raided the Tiv, he said, and the Tiv were powerless against them. Lives were lost. Property was looted. Women were raped. Those dastardly Udam!

But one Tiv man at that time, he went on, knew a regional government official of Tiv and could bend the ear of a person in power. That one in authority did a very good thing, said Yakubu. He ordered bulldozers to dig a huge open space in the jungle, sort of like a bunker silo. He called in the construction workers to pour a concrete slab floor. They raised some walls and strung some lights. They built a stage to accommodate a band.

Then the government man sent out invitations only to the highest-ranking leaders of the Udam tribe. "Come to my party!" said the invitations. "Come for the music! Come for the dancing! Come for the drinking!"

So they came, the leaders of the Udam tribe. They had a rousing night of partying. When it was over for the first night, the man in charge invited them back a second night. "Bring your friends!" he said. "Bring your relatives! Come back tomorrow night!"

So they did. No one wanted to miss a good party. Who could refuse a few drinks and some pretty women? This was the place to be! These were the people to be with. And the party got better every night. More music. More women. More food. More drinks.

By the end of the week, everybody who was anybody in the Udam tribe was crowded onto that concrete slab dance floor. Though no one could see it at first, this night was different. When the music swelled and the dancers swirled and the lights swayed, something new began to happen. Something awful. Something not soon to be forgotten.

Armed soldiers mysteriously appeared and lined the ridge above the dance floor. Suddenly their rifles spat fire in the night and logs soaked in kerosene rolled down the earthwork walls. Bodies were crushed and burned, and screams of horror tried to push back the vengeance. But it couldn't be stopped. That night the brightest and the best and the boldest of the Udam tribe laid dead under smoldering logs. In the morning the bulldozers returned to hide the carnage once again under the floor of the jungle.

When the Principal finished his story, nodding heads confirmed it. "That's what has to happen again!" said my gentle neighbor, steaming now with passion and power.

When I walked the dark path to our house that night, for one of the few times in my life, I was really scared. What was this place that I'd brought my family into? The power of evil nearly suffocated me.

Think of it. Here were ministers of the Gospel of Jesus Christ, plotting a revenge that exceeded the crime. They were talking of organizing the students of the school into a squadron of armed killers. And they relished a twice-told tale of lethal vengeance.

AN INNATE SENSE OF JUSTICE

Where does that come from? Where is this urgency for revenge born?

Jesus himself acknowledges that it's been around for a long time. "You know what we've been taught," he says. "An eye for an eye. A tooth for a tooth. That's the way things are in this world."

So it is, and we all know it. I once heard a story in Ontario of a farmer near London. His apple orchards line Highway 4, just south of the city. Every fall the same thing would happen. Cars would pull to the side of the road. People would jump out and raid his trees. Then they'd hop back over the fence, get in the car again, and speed away.

One day when it happened, though, he was ready. As the thieving family got back to the car, arms bulging with apples, they found the farmer leaning up against the fender. The family was rather sheepish.

Blushing, the father said to the farmer, "We hope you don't mind that we took a few of your apples."

"No, not at all," said the farmer. "I hope you don't mind that I took some of the air out of your tires."

Revenge comes easily for us. Manolo Ramos, of Barcelona, Spain, ran a nice little restaurant. But then a former acquaintance of Manolo's opened another restaurant, just down the street. So Ramos got the neighborhood kids together in the park and asked if they wanted to make a little money. He bought them some gum, gave them a few coins, and then told them to chew the gum and spit it out on the sidewalk in front of his competitor's restaurant.

But no one has a monopoly on vengeance. Ramos was subsequently arrested for his actions and is now facing two months in jail and a fine equivalent to $1,500 US. So it goes in our world.

In his classic, *Mere Christianity,* C. S. Lewis talks about the sense of vengeance that pervades our world. Lewis became a Christian on precisely this point. He says that it never ceased to amaze him how people of all cultures demand to have their rights protected. A child fights to hang on to a toy in the nursery. A man will attack you if you scratch the paint on his new car. A woman feeds the gossip network to get back at someone who wronged her. It's the stuff of the office scramble. It's the vicious competition schools and colleges foster. It's the thing societies hang their hats on, more and more.

Lewis says that the strength of moral indignation in the human soul astounded him as an atheist. He gradually came to realize that there had to be some sort of moral power at work in this universe, if vengeance was such an innate part of the human spirit. We may not live, at all times, according to the moral standards we espouse. Yet if someone else violates our rights, we cry "Foul!" to high heaven.

Where, asks Lewis, do we get that urgent sense of "our rights"? Where does it come from in the smallest child? Where is it fostered in every single culture on earth? Where do we get this idea, whether we claim to be religious or not, that we have an intrinsic right to certain things?

Lewis says that when he started to think about that, he began to believe in God. When he realized the depth of our moral indignation, he realized as well that it had to come from some power that transcends the system.

We cry "Foul!" because some higher power taught us the meaning of "Fair." And if that is so, even with our sinful tendencies, the need to repay an injustice is bred in our bones.

So here we are. We want to love others. But like the teachers of the Law in Jesus' day, we put our limits on love at exactly two points. We do not do good to our enemies because they are not really human, like us. And we do not think kindly on those who have violated our rights, because they have hurt us. Here the justice of the universe takes a firm stand. In righteous indignation we cry, "An eye for an eye! A tooth for a tooth!"

THE LOGIC OF GRACE

But somewhere here, the logic of vengeance breaks down. We all believe in justice; we all cry out to have our rights protected. Yet the power of revenge eventually takes us beyond where any of us truly want to go, for two reasons.

First of all, because of sin, we tend to be more zealous in our vindictiveness than we are in our love. I am much quicker to strike out at someone else and seek revenge against him for what he's done to me, than I am to be that righteous myself.

If I make a promise to you and I break it, I'll want you to brush it off lightly. I'll want you to say, "Never mind. That's okay." After all, in my way of thinking I've got a good excuse for breaking my promise.

But if *you* make a promise to *me*, and *you* fail to come through on it, I'm not going to let you get off so easily. You did me wrong, and I'm going to make sure you know that. I can't count on you. You're not very dependable, like *I* am.

That, says C. S. Lewis, is the way justice get perverted because of sin. I still have rights, but you don't.

The second reason the logic of vengeance breaks down is that the God who taught us justice has himself learned to temper it with mercy, and that's a lesson we too often haven't learned.

During a heated debate at a church's board meeting, one of the overwrought members jumped to his feet, clenched his fists, and yelled, "I have my rights!"

The air was charged. The battle lines were being drawn in people's minds. Then came this quiet word from one of the older men: "You don't really mean that. If we had our rights, we'd all be in hell."

It's true. Were justice alone to serve us in life, the march would be stern and mean, and the inn at the eve of the journey would be the infamous "Hotel California," where, according to legend and song, you can check in anytime, but you can never leave. Much better, according to the psalmist, is the place where God gathers us. There "love and faithfulness meet together; righteousness and peace kiss each other" (Psalm 85:10).

God knows how to temper his justice with the kiss of peace, but when it's time for us to show mercy, we're slow to the draw.

Sometimes people hurt us, but they think they're doing us good. I know a pastor and his wife who claim their oldest daughter was born early because a couple in their congregation thought they needed to set my friend straight on a few issues. My friend was a single man when he went to that congregation, but during his first years as pastor got married. After the newlyweds had been married a year, this other couple in his congregation, with all the righteousness of misguided saintly convictions, wrote them a nasty letter, complaining that the pastor's work had suffered because of his wife. The pastor and his wife went to the couple's house to talk about the allegations, even though the pastor's wife was almost nine months pregnant. Minister and spouse were rudely treated and, after more wild accusations, told to get out of the house. After a sleepless night the pastor's wife went into early labor.

Sometimes people hurt us because they have problems of their own. I've got a booklet of quotations on my desk, a gift from a woman I'll call Terry. Terry's first husband (whom I'll call Fred) was a nice guy, except when he got drunk. Then he became a monster. He beat her and tormented their two sons. Fred drained their bank account till Terry was penniless, and had to beg for a few leftovers from the neighbors. Terry's husband didn't mean to hurt her. He just did. Again and again.

Sometimes people hurt us by mistake. The Canadian Red Cross didn't test its blood for the HIV virus for *eight years* after the test was available. They didn't want to spend the money, and they didn't want to scare anybody. So today there are thousands of folks in Canada who die of AIDS, just because a couple people made a mistake.

Here's where the logic of revenge breaks down. Although we think striking back will take care of our hurt, ease our pain, and make the suffering go away, it never does. Vengeance is never sweet. It's poison. I know. I've got the poison in my veins. Often it seems it is killing me.

The power of vengeance erupted in our lives some years ago when Brenda's younger brother, Ken, died suddenly. The story behind that death is so twisted and horrible that we have a hard time reviewing it without screaming for revenge. Ken's death was a tragedy, complicated by a heap of injustices done to him and to all of us in the family by one person, and the logic of vengeance has eaten away at us all. I understand, now, just exactly what my Tiv friends had in mind when we sat that dark night in the hellish jungles of Nigeria.

There is a greater power than the energy of vengeance. There is a higher logic than the instinct of revenge. And even though I really don't think that's possible, I know it's true. I know it's true, because I have felt the power of love. I know it's true, because I have experienced the logic of grace, where justice and peace kiss, where righteousness and forgiveness embrace. In moments of grace, "I have been to the mountaintop," as Martin Luther King Jr. said, "and I have seen the glory of the coming of the Lord!"

A WORLD WAITING TO BE BORN

The great German preacher Helmut Thielicke preached a powerful sermon on Matthew 5:38–48 shortly after World War II when the Nazi beast was destroyed, and soon after he himself had survived unusual horrors at the hands of cruel men.

He called the message "No Retaliation." It was a message that Europe desperately needed to hear in the aftermath of the brutalities between nations that tore the continent apart.

In order to make Jesus' words come alive in human hearts, Thielicke told of a woman he knew whose husband was a beastly monster. He told of the cruelties she endured at his hands, and the indecencies she suffered from his mouth.

From a human point of view, he said, she despised him. There was nothing of forgiving grace left in her.

But then the change happened for her, says Thielicke. It happened one day in the middle of one of his wild tirades against her. Just as he was about to strike her again, and just as she was about to lash out in loathsome hatred, she saw him, in her mind's eye, only for an instant, as the loving young man she had married. In that moment she learned to love him again. From that moment on, whenever he was at his worst, she would remember him at his best, and in that remembering she would forgive him. She could forgive him.

"That," said Thielicke, "is what we each must learn to do!"

I'd like to agree with him. I'd like to say, "Yes, that's the way. That's how we take hold of Jesus' teaching." But I can't, because it doesn't work for me. I can't see any good in the person who is so responsible for the tragedy of Ken's death. I've truly tried. That person seems to me to be one of the folks that M. Scott Peck wrote about in his powerful book *The People of the Lie* (New York: Simon & Schuster, 1983). Some folks, Peck writes, seem to be sold to evil in ways beyond our ability to understand or to correct or to live with.

But C. S. Lewis says I have to live with myself, and I have to learn to love myself, even though I don't always like who I am or what I do.

He said that forgiveness begins when we learn to wish for others something good, in much the same way that we wish for ourselves something of goodness that grows beyond the evil inside. I may not always like who I am, I may not always appreciate what I do, but, by the grace of God, I do wish good for myself in spite of my faults and failures.

And isn't that the picture that Jesus gives us of God? "Look," says Jesus, "He causes the sun to rise on the evil and the good. He sends rain on the righteous and the unrighteous." In other words, the world God is opening up to us is a world in which he wishes to bring something good to us in spite of ourselves. In spite of who we are. In spite of what we do to each other. In spite of what justice alone might dictate.

Here is the beginning of grace: not in our ability to remember some faint spark of goodness in people who have become monsters to us, but in our ability to wish them the good we hope God will one day bring to us. Not because they deserve it. But because this is where life begins.

Lewis Smedes tells of his friend Myra Broger. Myra, says Smedes, is an actress and a beautiful woman. A few years ago she was nearly killed by a hit-and-run driver. Now she's crippled.

At the time of the accident, she was married to another actor, a TV and film star. He stayed with Myra long enough to see that she didn't die from the accident. Then he divorced her. He couldn't be encumbered by her crippled weight. He's off with other women who aren't crippled.

Myra hated him, of course. She hated him for what he did to her. She hated him for the vows he broke, and for the meanness that left her alone, just when she needed him most.

Lew Smedes asked her one time if she had ever been able to forgive him. After she thought about it for a while she nodded her head with slow deliberation. Yes, she thought she had begun to forgive him.

Smedes was curious. How did she come to that conclusion? How could she tell if she had forgiven him?

Myra replied, "I find myself wishing him well." Just that simple.

Smedes was unsure. Could this really be the case? He probed further by asking a pointed question. "Myra, suppose you learned today that he had married a sexy young starlet. Could you pray that he would be happy with her?"

Smedes says that he expected her to bristle at the thought, but she didn't. She responded almost casually, he says, and she told him, "Yes, I could and I would. Steve needs love very much, and I want him to have it."

That's not a blazing declaration of absolution for his crimes, but it is a crack in hell's armor. As I sat at my desk reflecting on these words of Jesus I asked myself about my relationship with the person in our own story of Ken's tragedy. Do I wish that person any good in life? Do I desire for that person any of the grace of God? Do I hope the sunshine falls on that person in any moment of delight?

It's a moment of truth we all have to face, for not one of us can walk away from Jesus' words without a good hard look in the mirror. After all, when the scales of justice are balanced on Judgment Day, it will be love that gathers all God's children home. On that day no one will clamor for revenge, and then we will be so thankful that love never kept to the safety of heaven. For Love took the form of a servant. Nothing should have been done to Love that was done to him. It was a hideous way to treat the kindness of God. Yet Love endured the wrongs and unleashed the powers of a world waiting to be born.

The evidence is seen in lives like yours. Remember Blake's words:

> Love seeketh not itself to please,
> Nor for itself hath any care,
> But for another gives its ease,
> And builds a Heaven in Hell's despair.

"Be careful not to do your 'acts of righteousness' before men, to be seen by them. If you do, you will have no reward from your Father in heaven.

"So when you give to the needy, do not announce it with trumpets, as the hypocrites do in the synagogues and on the streets, to be honored by men. I tell you the truth, they have received their reward in full. But when you give to the needy, do not let your left hand know what your right hand is doing, so that your giving may be in secret. Then your Father, who sees what is done in secret, will reward you."

—Matthew 6:1–4

8
A PORTION OF THYSELF

Passing the Goods Without Passing the Buck

THE PRESIDENT of the college I attended was the kind of man who always said what was on his mind. He had a very healthy self-image and wasn't concerned about how people might take him. At one of the graduation ceremonies, he stood at the podium, looked out over the huge crowd of people, shook his head, and said to himself (right into the microphone, of course), "All these Christians in one place, and no one's taking an offering!"

We take offerings a lot, don't we? Every Sunday when Christians gather for worship, the collection plates are passed. In fact, rarely does a gathering of Christians pass where there isn't some suggestion about offerings or donations or contributions.

Someone told me the story of an airplane flight where one of the engines had failed and another was sputtering. The passengers were fearful, and some began to panic. Finally one fellow sitting near the front of the plane yelled, "Is there a priest or a minister on board who can do something religious?" Dutifully, a clergyman got up, and passed his hat for an offering.

Money and religion often go hand in hand.

And maybe they should. They certainly did for Jesus. The gospels record thirty-seven of his parables, and in sixteen, Jesus talks about money and the way in which we use our possessions.

Moreover, one-tenth of all the verses in the gospels deal directly with the subject of money. That's 288 verses. When you look at the whole Bible, you find that less than five hundred verses speak specifically about faith, and only five hundred verses talk about prayer, yet more than two thousand verses address money and possessions.

Religion and money go hand in hand. Of course, that's essentially what Jesus is saying in these verses. Your faith and your finances are part of the same package. What you do with your checkbook is as important as what you do with your Bible.

Maybe pop icon Madonna wasn't far from the truth when she sang, "We're living in a material world and I am a material girl." If that is the case, and if our material substance matters to God as much as it matters to us, there are several questions we have to face on a regular basis.

ARE YOU AWARE?

First: Are you aware? Do you see others around you? Has your faith opened your eyes to the need and the concerns of your partners in the human race?

Probably no period in human history was as peaceful and as prosperous as the days of Antonius Pious (A. D. 138–161), who ruled Rome in the second century. Edward Gibbon, in his magnificent treatise *The Decline and Fall of the Roman Empire,* said that the times of Antonius Pious were the happiest on earth. He was probably right. There was more wealth, business success, and domestic peace in those days than most civilizations have ever known.

Antonius Pious was a good ruler, and his people knew it. In fact, one of his biggest supporters was the Athenian philosopher Aristedes. Aristedes couldn't seem to write enough verses in praise of Antonius. He lauded the government and the beauty of Rome. He praised the magnificence of its buildings and the character of its citizens. Aristedes was a one-man ministry of propaganda, telling the world of the pomp and splendor of Antonius Pious and his great government.

But Aristedes wrote about other things as well. One day he sent a letter to Antonius, telling the monarch to keep his eye on a certain group of people in his empire. "You need these people," said Aristedes. "You should find them and talk with them. You can learn much from them."

The unique thing about them, said Aristedes, is that they really have eyes to see others. They watch out for those around them. They take care of the widows, who are often pushed aside when their husbands die. They look after orphans, especially those who get sold as slaves. These people will even pay huge sums of money to buy the freedom of others.

It's not that these folks are so wealthy. In fact, said Aristedes, they are often the poorest of most Roman cities. Yet if they know of someone in need, they will even go without food for two or three days in order to save a few coins that might help someone else.

"You should get to know these people, Antonius!" said Aristedes. "In all your grand empire they are the only ones who make it a habit to see the needs of the poor and do something about it."

Who was Aristedes writing about? Christians. He was writing about the followers of Jesus. Can you imagine it? A Greek philosopher, telling one of the greatest Roman emperors to look for Christians because they were the ones from whom he could learn something.

Jesus asks if we have learned that lesson. Are we aware? Do we see? Have we reached beyond ourselves and looked at the lives and the circumstances of our partners in the human enterprise?

One of the greatest statements about Jesus comes in a story that is told by all four of the gospel writers. Jesus was at the end of a busy day. People demanded a lot from him. He was tired from traveling around and talking with the crowds. In his humanity, he had been drained by the many sick who came to him begging to be healed.

When it grew late, the disciples wanted to send the crowds away. They should go home, so Jesus could find a place to rest for the night. But the gospel writers tell us Jesus looked at the people around him, and he had compassion on them, and then he gave them food and rest.

He looked. He saw. He felt. He touched.

Do we share his character? Do we see the needs of those around us? Can we feel the hurts throbbing through the world? Are we aware?

In 1966, evangelist Martin Higgenbottem was one of the main speakers at the Berlin World Congress on Evangelism. He told the gathering that his life of devotion and service was inspired by his mother. He remembered coming home from school one afternoon to find her sitting at the kitchen table with a strange man. The fellow was obviously someone who lived on the streets. His clothes were filthy, his hair was slicked with unwashed grease, and he smelled of a mixture of unkind odors.

Martin's mother was chatting pleasantly with him while he devoured a plate of sandwiches. She had gone shopping that morning and found him cold and hungry, so she brought him home with her.

When the man was ready to leave, he said passionately, "I wish there were more people in the world like you."

Martin's mother casually threw the compliment aside. "Oh," she said, "there are. You just have to look for them."

The man broke down. He shook his head, and tears rolled across his cheeks. "But lady," he said, "I didn't have to look for you. You looked for me."

WILL YOU SHARE?

A second question follows: Will you share? Will you take what you have and give to those around you? Will you use your blessings to touch the lives of others?

A wonderful story is told about Fiorello La Guardia, mayor of New York City during the Great Depression. Before he became mayor, he served for a time as a police court judge. One cold winter's day they brought a man to him who was charged with stealing a loaf of bread. La Guardia asked him if he was guilty. The man nodded. He had taken the bread because his family was starving, and he had no money to buy food.

"I've got to punish you," he told the man. "The law makes no exceptions. I fine you ten dollars!" He brought down his gavel.

But where would the man get the money for the fine? Now they would have to throw him in jail as well.

La Guardia wasn't finished, though. He already had his hand on his wallet. He pulled out ten dollars, handed it to the bailiff and said, "Here's the money for your fine."

Then he took back the ten dollars, put it into a hat, handed the hat to the bailiff and said, "I'm going to suspend the sentence, and I'm going to fine everyone here in the courtroom fifty cents for living in a town where a man has to steal bread in order to eat."

When the man left the courtroom that day, he had the light of life in his eyes and $47.50 in his pocket.

Will you share what God has given you with others around who have needs?

It was a requirement of the Jewish religion to give alms for the poor. That's what Jesus is talking about in Matthew 6:1–4. In fact, the Old Testament rules and regulations had a built-in system that guaranteed help for the poor. You were not even allowed to come to the temple for worship unless you had given alms to the poor.

Tithing was a standard practice. One-tenth of everything you earned was to be given back to God as a confession of faith. But how can you give money to God? Do the deacons take the offerings and go into the back room of the church and toss it all up to heaven, and whatever God doesn't want falls back to the floor? No, God's instructions were very clear. When you give your tithes to the poor, he said, you are giving them to me.

Jesus echoes that idea in a later teaching. In Matthew 25 he talks about the end of time and the day we will all appear before the throne of God for judgment. God will say to some, "You took care of me. When I was hungry, you fed me. When I was naked, you clothed me. When I was sick, you looked after me."

We'll shake our heads, says Jesus, and have this puzzled look on our faces. We'll say to God, "When was that? I don't remember ever seeing you on earth. When did we help you like that?"

The Father will look at us, says Jesus, and he will answer, "When you gave to the poor among you, when you offered help to those who needed it, when you went beyond yourself in mercy, I counted it as if you did it to me."

We don't always do well at that, do we? The Internal Revenue Service tells us that Americans give about 1.65 percent of their incomes to charity. That includes *all* charitable causes, like the arts and universities and hospitals and cultural centers. If the goal is to give one-tenth of one's income, that means almost 85 percent of the tithe is missing.

It's not that we are isolated from the needs in our world. We hear the news, we see the pictures, and we're challenged by the requests that come every day in the mail. When Jesus asks if we are aware, we can only say, "Yes, painfully so."

But when Jesus asks, "Will you share?" that's a different story. We are programmed to take, rather than give. We are taught by our society to receive, but not necessarily to share. We are challenged by our age to grab for all the gusto we can get, and not to deprive ourselves of anything for the sake of others.

John Bright, a British politician of the nineteenth century, was walking down a street one day when a fellow was seriously injured in an accident. The crowds gathered around, gasping in delighted horror at the blood and gore. But Bright took off his hat, grabbed a ten-pound note from his wallet, and stuffed it into his hat. Then he pushed his way through the crowds and said, "I'm ten pounds sorry for this man! How sorry are you?"

In moments he had turned the sickening curiosity of the people into sympathetic compassion.

Are you aware? Will you share?

Those are Jesus' questions for us.

DO YOU CARE?

Then comes the most important question of all. Do you care? Do you really care about others? Is compassion a way of life for you?

Helmut Thielicke tells of a time he was hospitalized and in great pain. The nurses were wonderful and took great care of him. One nurse in particular impressed him. She worked the night shift. Every evening she was there—prompt, pleasant, efficient. She seemed to care deeply about her patients. She always had a bright smile for them.

In fact, in the sleepless hours of the night, she often sat next to Thielicke and talked with him. For twenty years she had been on this shift. For twenty years she had worked while others slept. She had given of herself in the darkest hours of the night.

"Isn't it a pretty stressful thing for you?" Thielicke asked her. "Don't you ever get tired of it all? How do you keep it up, year after year?

"She beamed at me," Thielicke explained, "and said, 'Well, you see, every night that I work sets another jewel in my heavenly crown. I've already got 7,175 in a row.'"

Thielicke was stunned. His gratitude toward her evaporated. She didn't really care about him. She wasn't helping him through his tough times because she felt compassion for him. She was only doing this in order to earn some kind of reward. Every night she kept count of her good deeds. Every smile was sold at a price. Every shift was merely a deposit in the bank of heaven.

Sure, she was aware. Yes, she was willing to share. But did she care? Did her heart go with the gift? Did her spirit reach with her fingers and touch the one she tended? Apparently not, thought Thielicke.

It is true that Jesus talks about the rewards we get from God for the gifts of charity we give during our lives. Yet rewards come in several different forms. Sometimes they are tacked on at the end of our achievements, like birthday presents. A student may get a car from her parents when she graduates from high school. The car and the education are not directly related, and if the gift is used as an incentive to make passing grades, it can but does not necessarily promote learning.

Another kind of reward might be a personal computer. Such a graduation gift would affirm more closely the value of a student's work. The parents' desire with such a reward might be to say, "You've done a great job in high school. Here's something that will help you as you continue your studies at college."

A third type of reward is far more difficult to define, yet most valuable of all. It is the reward of experiencing the fulfillment of the work itself. The reward might be the pleasure of having a conversation with a Paris waiter in a sidewalk cafe after years of French classes. It might be the relief of saving a child's life in a hospital emergency room when first certified as a doctor. Such rewards extend the exercise of our duty into the quality of our lives themselves.

In this manner Jesus' talk of rewards for charity is something far from crass or dirty. One might try, of course, to get richer by being charitable. Several years ago a man in Florida brought a lawsuit against his church. He demanded that it return to him the $800 that he had contributed the year before. His court documents included this testimony:

> On September 7 I delivered $800 of my savings to the ______ church in response to the pastor's promise that blessings, benefits, and reward would come to the person who tithed his wealth. I did not and have not received these benefits.

You foolish man, Jesus would say. You silly beggar. Do you give in order to get? Do you tithe to earn a profit? Do you offer your services on the floor of the trading markets?

Sir Roger L'Estrange writes, "He that serves God for money will serve the Devil for better wages." He is right. That is exactly Jesus' point. Those who trumpet their gifts to get temporal honors or social significance will reap the rewards they desire. But those who learn the caring heart of God will find a return far more significant. They will experience the thrill of grace that makes them more like the Father himself.

We are tempted, though, by rewards of the first order. So often we ask, "What's in it for me? What do I get out of it? Will anybody notice? Do I get the Good Citizen of the Year award? Will there be a write-up in the papers?"

One man I know served in the church all his life. Now, in his senior years, however, he has become bitter. Nobody has ever really thanked him. None of the younger people in the church realize how much he has given. So he pulls back and wraps himself in a security blanket of self-pity.

One woman's face was wet with tears when she came to see me. All these years she has volunteered her time and talents. Other women went out and got jobs and earned money. But she always felt it was her responsibility to visit the needy, to make meals for the poor, and to call on the sick at the hospital every week. Now she is tired of it all. Nobody cares what she has done. Nobody has ever stood up and thanked her publicly. Why should she give any more of herself if people are so ungracious?

Why indeed? If that's what it's all about, why indeed?

In C. S. Lewis' sermon "The Weight of Glory," he talks about the idea of rewards in the Christian faith. God promises us a reward for what we do in his name. But that doesn't make us mercenaries, giving in order to get, selling our good deeds on the open market.

If a man would marry a woman with great wealth in order to get her money, said Lewis, we would call him mercenary, and rightly so. We would thumb our noses at him and be appalled at his audacity.

But if a man marries a rich woman only because he expects the reward of love, says Lewis, we would think him the greatest fellow on earth. He would be getting his reward, but it would actually be the fulfillment of what he is himself giving to the other. His reward is the extension of his gift.

So it is with us, says Lewis. We give of ourselves in Christian charity. We give of our time, our talents, and our money. And, as Jesus says, God will reward us.

But what will that reward be? A million dollars? A life without sickness or cancer? A public declaration of our good deeds?

No.

The reward is simply to become one with Love itself, to give as we have been given, to share in the delights of his sharing, to stretch our souls and to find ourselves.

"I think," says Annie Dillard, "that the dying prayer at last is not 'please,' but 'thank you,' as a guest thanks his host at the door."

She is right. At its best, life on earth is not about a demand for recognition, but a quiet "thank you" for all that we have been able to see and show and share.

That doesn't necessarily make good copy in the morning newspaper. Nor does it necessarily mean that we will be successful in life, at least in the ways many count success.

King Oswin, an early ruler of a northern territory in Britain, once gave his prize stallion to the local bishop as a token of appreciation. As the bishop traveled, he met a beggar along the road. Since the man had nothing at all, the bishop got off his fine steed and put the reigns in the man's hand. "Take him!" ordered the bishop. "Sell him and live. He's all I have to give you."

When King Oswin found out what the bishop had done he said, "Why didn't you send him to me? We have dozens of old horses that are more fitting for a beggar."

The bishop quietly asked, "Is that stallion worth more than a child of God?"

King Oswin thought about the question for a moment and suddenly threw off his royal robes, fell at the bishop's feet, and cried to God for forgiveness. The bishop blessed him and sent him away in peace. But for a long time, he stared after the king with sorrowful eyes. When one asked him why he was so troubled, bishop Adrian replied, "I know that the king will not live long, for I have never seen a king as humble as he is. He will be taken from us, as the country is not worthy to have such a king."

His words proved true. In A.D. 651 the king was murdered by a neighboring rival who used Oswin's own kindness to gain an audience. And the world was poorer that day.

But you are still here, and I am still here. And today we can read again the questions Jesus asks in these verses.

Are you aware? Do you see the needs of others around you? Are your eyes open to the plight of the poor and the troubles of the destitute?

Will you share? Will you take whatever God has given you and put it at the disposal of others? Will you see your goods and property as a loan on deposit from God to be shared in his name as others call for it?

Do you care? That is most important. Says Ralph Waldo Emerson, "Rings and jewels are not gifts, but apologies for gifts. The only gift is a portion of thyself." Is that the gift you give? Does your heart stretch out with the love of Jesus? Does compassion flow in your veins? Have you found his reward in the act of love?

"And when you pray, do not be like the hypocrites, for they love to pray standing in the synagogues and on the street corners to be seen by men. I tell you the truth, they have received their reward in full. But when you pray, go into your room, close the door and pray to your Father, who is unseen. Then your Father, who sees what is done in secret, will reward you. And when you pray, do not keep on babbling like pagans, for they think they will be heard because of their many words. Do not be like them, for your Father knows what you need before you ask him.

"This, then, is how you should pray:

"'Our Father in heaven,
hallowed be your name,
your kingdom come,
your will be done
    on earth as it is in heaven.
Give us today our daily bread.
Forgive us our debts,
    as we also have forgiven our debtors.
And lead us not into temptation,
but deliver us from the evil one.'

For if you forgive men when they sin against you, your heavenly Father will also forgive you. But if you do not forgive men their sins, your Father will not forgive your sins."

—Matthew 6:5–15

9
PROPER PRAYER

E-mail Protocol at www.heaven.com

IN AN ARTICLE about prayer, Jim Grant told about a business associate who had a particular weakness for sweets and fatty foods. The fellow had a problem controlling his weight. Every so often, he would announce that he was going on a diet once again.

Since he had to drive right past a bakery on his way to work each morning, a diet took will power. No matter what he tried to tell himself, his car somehow managed to smell the fresh aroma and would turn by itself into the bakery parking lot. What could he do? Almost every morning he arrived at the office with a bag of doughnuts or a box of pastries.

This new diet was going to be different, however. The man was really serious this time. He even traveled to work on alternate streets just to avoid the bakery. Everyone at the office was skeptical at first but gradually began to cheer him along in hope.

But that all crashed one morning when the dieter walked into the office carrying a huge, heavily glazed coffee cake. Everyone groaned in exasperation and scolded him. What had happened?

"This is a very special coffee cake," the man replied. "I accidentally drove by the bakery this morning, and there was a sign in the window: 'We've baked a cake today just for you!' I thought that might be a message for me, but I wasn't sure, so I prayed. I said, 'Lord, if you want me to have that cake, let there be a parking space for me right in front of the door!'

"Sure enough! After I circled the block eight times, there it was!"

Isn't that like us? We want a God who hears our prayers, and who is powerful enough to change things for us, but we really don't want him to be in control. We really don't want him to take over or to have his ways rule our lives.

For that reason prayer can be difficult for us, and Jesus knows that. That is why he talked to his disciples and gave them patterns and ideas for prayer.

WHY DO YOU WANT TO PRAY?

In a sense, the first thing Jesus does, is ask a question. "Why do you want to pray?" he seems to say. We might put it like this, "What do you hope to get out of your prayers?"

That is a good question. Have you ever thought about how foolish prayer looks? Did you ever see a television program or a movie where they made prayer look normal or fitting or perfectly reasonable? It never seems to happen.

I think of Paul Schrader, who grew up in a Christian Reformed home in Grand Rapids, Michigan, and attended Calvin College. Then he became a major Hollywood movie director and producer. Some years ago he made a movie about a teenaged girl who got caught up in the pornography world of southern California.

She started out in a normal home. She was a good kid, a Christian girl from a church-going family. The film begins on Thanksgiving Day with the relatives gathered for a turkey dinner. The feast is on the table, and they turn off the television set just long enough for the father, played by George C. Scott, to pray.

When he bows his head to say a few trite words to some unseen being, it is almost embarrassing. Is that what it looks like when we pray at mealtime? Paul Schrader seems to think so. He grew up with that nonsense—here we are, barely pausing, hardly turning down the volume of the TV, using language that is strange and archaic, fidgeting until it's all done.

It's not a pretty picture.

Why do we pray? Is there any sense behind it?

Jesus indicates that there were a lot of different reasons why the people in his day prayed. Many of those reasons were not all that great.

Here's a fellow, says Jesus, who puts on a show for others. He prays to convince them that he's religious. He knows all the right words. He has just the right tone. He can make you feel so good, so spiritual, when you listen to him pray.

It reminds me of a young woman who came to me years ago with doubts about her Christian faith. She didn't know if she was faking her faith or if she really believed in God.

Her parents were leaders in their church, so I asked her if she had talked with them about these things. "No!" she said emphatically. "They're part of the problem."

Her father always led in prayer at meal time, she told me. Often they would invite others to join them for dinner. But whenever the minister or some other "important" person would be there, her dad would launch into a prayer of heavenly proportions. It was twice as high, three times as deep, four times as wide, and five times as long as usual. The whole time he prayed, she said, she and her brothers and sisters smothered sniggers and kicked each other under the table.

That's the kind of Christianity she grew up with. Looking back, she wasn't sure whether she truly had any faith herself. Maybe it was all a show, all a pretense. Maybe she only acted like a Christian in order to impress others. It had been a long time since she felt like praying. When she did, she wasn't even sure why she prayed anymore.

Have you ever felt like her?

Jesus points to other folks. Prayer for them, he indicates, is a bit like magic. They figure that if they just pray long enough about something, and if they just keep at it persistently enough, they will surely get what they want.

In my home community in Minnesota, a boy in third grade came home one day to find that his grandfather had just died. The next day one of his classmates told him, "You didn't pray enough. If your family had more faith, your grandpa wouldn't have died."

Where would a third grade student get an idea like that? Whatever would possess a little person to say such a terrible thing?

Probably it came from his home. His parents talked that way, and he just passed it along. Prayer, for them, was a magical lantern, or a menu of divine treats on sale for the right price. Just say the right words, just pray long enough, and God will give you what you want. You can even keep your grandfather alive longer.

Appalling, isn't it? But we all think that way at times.

One of the managers of a successful business in London, Ontario, used to stop by my office every couple of weeks. He had gotten himself into some particular problems, and he figured that if a minister would pray for him, God would work things out better than if he only prayed on his own. So he came to me for prayer.

One time he told me that he visited a number of ministers around the city and had them all praying for him. He was certain that God had to help him now, seeing that so many ministers were praying for him. For him, prayer was magic that happened when you got the right people to say the right things the right number of times in the right way.

I like the way Bill Keane put it one time in his *Family Circus* comic strip. Little Jeffy picked up his football, and looked forlorn because it was flat. A car had run over it. Little Jeffy says to himself, "I need a new football! I don't know if I should send up a prayer, write a letter to Santa Claus, or call Grandma!"

What should he do? What would you do? Do you know the difference?

Why *do* you pray? Have you thought about it? What does prayer mean to you?

WHY SHOULD YOU WANT TO PRAY?

That brings us to the next question: what is prayer really all about?

Jesus answers by saying that when we want to pray, we should go to our rooms, close the door, and talk with our Father as if he were an old friend.

I remember Sunday afternoons when I was a boy. I would invite a friend over, and after lunch, if it was too cold to be outside, we would go up to my bedroom. We'd flop down on my bed and talk about all kinds of things.

That's the picture Jesus paints for us here. In the houses of his day most of the work and business and social activities would take place outside in the courtyard. If you invited a close friend to come over, however, you would take your friend into the inner rooms of your house. You would go to a place where it was quiet and private, where you could sit around and enjoy each other's company.

Ralph Waldo Emerson tells of a visit to his good friend Thomas Carlyle. Thomas met him at the door with a pipe in his mouth and an extra pipe in his hand. Emerson said that his friend shook his hand, gave him the extra pipe, lit it, and then led him to a cozy room. The fireplace was crackling softly, and they sat in chairs facing the glow. Emerson reports that they sat together there for several hours, hardly saying anything, just enjoying the warmth and the friendship and the camaraderie.

Late in the evening when Emerson stood to leave, the two of them had exchanged few words but had spent one of the most enjoyable times together that either could remember.

Something like that might well be what Jesus has in mind when he talks about going to meet God in a secret place. He's not saying that we should never pray in public, nor that we should take the prayers out of our churches and schools and family gatherings. Instead, he is trying to tell us that prayer is really a conversation between friends. It's the talk that deepens a bond of care. Friends don't need always to look at each other when they talk. They can walk side by side. They can stand together looking out over the ocean. They can sit on a park bench and watch the squirrels at play.

When we view prayer like that, it doesn't seem so strange anymore. Who cares if you can't see God? Is that so important? You sense his presence. You know his tenderness. You feel his power. For that reason, you carry on a conversation with him like you would walking with a friend in the dark.

The story is told of a young girl who lost her playmate, Jennifer, in a tragic auto accident. The day after the funeral, the young girl disappeared for several hours. When she finally came home, her mother asked her where she had been.

"I went to Jennifer's place," she said, "and I helped her mommy."

"How did you help Jennifer's mom?"

"Well," she said, "neither of us knew what to do, so I just crawled into her lap and helped her cry."

That might be as good a picture as any to summarize what Jesus is saying about prayer. Two friends laughing together. Crying together. Chatting together. Quiet together. That's prayer. That's what you do in your room together.

When you think about it, the model prayer Jesus gave us doesn't really match up to many of the other great prayers of the Bible. Think of Solomon's prayer at the dedication of the Temple. Now that was a great prayer!

Or read the marvelous prayer of David in Psalm 139:1–2,7, 23–24:

> O LORD, you have searched me
> and you know me.
> You know when I sit and when I rise;
> you perceive my thoughts from afar. . . .
> Where can I go from your Spirit?
> Where can I flee from your presence? . . .
> Search me, O God, and know my heart;
> test me and know my anxious thoughts.
> See if there is any offensive way in me,
> and lead me in the way everlasting.

There's a prayer for every human heart.

And reflect on other powerful prayers—Daniel's passionate plea for his people, Paul's marvelous prayers in his letter to the Ephesian Christians. The Bible is full of great prayers. This teaching prayer by Jesus doesn't really seem to match the others in power or impact or emotional strength. In fact, it almost whimpers to a close: "And lead us not into temptation, but deliver us from the evil one." That's it. That's all. Now you're done.

So what's so great about the Lord's Prayer? It's rather simple; there's not much to it. But maybe that's the point. It's not flowery. It doesn't use big words. It isn't grandiose. It really says only two things: "I hope things go well for you, God!" and "These are the things that I'm worried about!" Just those two things.

But isn't that essentially the conversation of friends? Isn't that the talk of those who know each other well?

Why should we pray? Maybe just to confirm and deepen and strengthen our relationship with God. Maybe just to chat awhile as friends do.

Does that mean we shouldn't ask God for anything? Not at all. When you have a need or a problem, it's your friend you go to first. You ask your friend for help, not a stranger. You ask those who know you best to assist you. That's a part of prayer.

One writer tells of a kindergarten class that took a field trip to the fire station. A firefighter was telling the children what to do in case of a fire. "First you go to the door," he said, "and you feel it to see if it's hot. Then you get down on your knees. Does anyone here know why you do that?"

"Sure," said one of the little ones. "You get down on your knees to ask God to get you out of this mess!"

That's certainly a part of prayer.

WHAT HAPPENS TO ME WHEN I PRAY?

There's one more little thing that Jesus adds at the end of these conversations. He says that prayer changes us. When we grow in our prayer life with God, we change within ourselves. We learn to live like God. We learn to talk like God. We learn to like the things that God likes and do the things that God does.

That's what Jesus' words about forgiving others mean. You can't carry on a conversation with a loving, forgiving God and not become a more loving, forgiving person. The two go hand in hand.

Someone has written something similar in a wonderful little tale called "The Happy Hypocrite." A rather crass and godless fellow spends his years using women and tossing them aside. One day he meets another young lady who catches his attention. She'll be his next conquest. Would she go out with him? Yes, if he would care to come to church with her.

Go to church? Well, if that's what it takes, he'll do it this one time. So he puts on some Sunday clothes, and he covers the evil lines of his face with a pious mask, and he begins again with his usual flirtation.

This time, however, something happens to him. He can't seem to take advantage of this young woman. He begins to respect her too much. They become friends, and lovers, and he even finds himself thinking of marriage.

Yet would she marry him if she knew what he was *really* like under this pious mask that he's worked so hard to keep in place? He's sure she would despise him if she found him out, so he keeps his mask in place. He hides the evil within, and he pretends to live in her good world, with all of its love and its joy and its religion.

Eventually they marry. They buy a house. They have children. And somehow he manages to keep his mask in place. He's a hypocrite, and he knows it, an evil man living in a world where he doesn't belong.

Still, over the years he finds that he likes this world of hers, and his mask begins to sit more comfortably on his face. He is ready to play this game until his dying day and live out his years as a happy hypocrite in this new world.

Then tragedy strikes. A woman from his early years finds him, someone he once used and scorned. Now she's ready for revenge. She'll expose him. She'll rip off his mask and show the world what he's really like. She'll uncover his hypocrisy, and his wife and children will be shattered.

They struggle together. She grabs for his mask and pulls it off his face, but then drops it, startled. The evil lines are gone. The hardness in his cheeks has softened. His face looks just like the pious mask.

He has lived in his wife's world so long that he's become part of it. For years his face was hidden by a mask of hypocrisy, but now he's become what she was for him: a friend, a lover, a kind and committed person. In fact, the happy hypocrite is a hypocrite no more.

That's what happens when you pray. You start out trying to impress God with your big words, trying to twist his arm with your magic formulas, trying to get him to notice you with your repetition. But along the way, you suddenly find that you've become friends. You've grown together. You start resembling him. In the end, prayer becomes less of a form than a conversation; less of a magical power than the dialogue of friends, or the silence of lovers.

Several decades ago a young woman found these concepts becoming real in her life. One night she wrote a prayer, putting her feelings into poetry. Later she composed a lilting melody that soared with beauty. During her last year of college, her choir director asked if she would sing the song on a recording he was producing.

I can still hear her voice lifting this moving prayer in the quiet innocence of love:

> God who touches earth with beauty, make me lovely too.
> With your Spirit recreate me, make my heart anew.
> Like the streams of living water make me crystal pure.
> Like the rocks of towering grandeur make me strong and sure.
> Like the dancing waves in sunlight make me glad and free.
> Like the straightness of the pine tree, let me upright be.
> Like the arches of the heaven lift my thoughts above.
> Turn my thoughts to noble actions, ministries of love.
> God who touches earth with beauty, make me lovely too.
> Keep me ever, by your Spirit, pure and strong and true.

"When you fast, do not look somber as the hypocrites do, for they disfigure their faces to show men they are fasting. I tell you the truth, they have received their reward in full. But when you fast, put oil on your head and wash your face, so that it will not be obvious to men that you are fasting, but only to your Father, who is unseen; and your Father, who sees what is done in secret, will reward you."

—*Matthew 6:16–18*

10
INTERNAL MEDICINE

A Crazy "Diet" that Might Actually Work!

SOME YEARS AGO, *Europa Times* carried a story in which Mussa Zoabi of Israel claimed to be the oldest person alive at 160. *Guinness Book of World Records* would not print his name, however, simply because his age could not be verified. Mr. Zoabi was older than most record-keeping systems.

Whatever his true age, Mussa Zoabi believed he knew the secret of longevity. He said, "Every day I drink a cup of melted butter or olive oil."

Doesn't *that* sound like a great diet?

Diets are quite the rage. Everybody has a special one. This diet can cure cancer. Another promises to reduce your weight, and then to keep those extra pounds off.

Already in ancient times there were diets that supposedly turned on the sex hormones and made a person irresistible. Now there's a report from Copenhagen that the Danes have a diet craze on their hands. People are eating horse food. Defenders of the diet ask, "You don't see many sick horses, do you?" Health Department spokesperson Haagen Schmidt says that "especially young women keep on eating hay and raw oats." They do it, he says, in spite of a tremendous surge in digestive problems reported by hospitals all over the country.

Sixty percent of women in North America say they're on a diet. A woman who works at Weight Watchers said that a new client had just begun the program. When she came in to be weighed after the first stressful week she stepped on the scale and found that she had lost a couple of pounds. The dieter wasn't too happy, however. She complained, "My friend comes here to Weight Watchers, and she said she lost ten pounds her first week! She told me I'd lose ten pounds in the first week too! But look at this!"

The leader at Weight Watchers was a little disturbed. She knew that you don't lose weight overnight, so she tried to comfort the woman by reminding her that the ideal was a slow weight loss. Following the Weight Watchers program was more likely to produce permanent weight reductions. She asked the dieter, a little indignantly, "Who told you that she lost ten pounds in her first week? Is she a doctor?"

The woman shook her head.

"Is she a nurse?"

"No," answered the woman.

"Is she a nutritionist, or another Weight Watchers leader?"

Negative again.

"Well who is she?"

"I think . . ." said the newcomer, ". . . I think she's a liar!"

Most of us know the truth and the lies about dieting. For that reason, we think we know all about the issue of fasting that Jesus raises. Fasting sounds a lot like dieting. You stop eating for a while, or at least you slow down, and you do it for a noble cause, even if it is just to fit into those slacks again.

In one of his letters C. S. Lewis writes, "Perhaps if we had done more voluntary fasting before, God would not now have to put us on these darn diets!"

Maybe so. In fact, earlier this century, Bernarr Macfadden, who had a wide following in North America, said that everybody should fast now and then, if only for the good health that it brings. Still, fasting is *not* dieting.

Neither is fasting like the hunger strikes we read about now and again. Comedian Dick Gregory, for instance, used to stage hunger strikes in protest of the Vietnam War. The mayor of Cork, Ireland, died of a hunger strike against English rule in the 1920s, giving rise to much larger protests. History repeated itself in the 1980s when Irish political prisoners in Maze Prison, near Belfast, carried on widely publicized hunger strikes. Several died in their protests against England. Again, during the days of the Cold War when tension tightened in the old Soviet Union, some of the Jewish people who weren't able to get exit visas went on hunger strikes. The media turned on the spotlights, and the Soviet government was forced to comply.

While it is true that hunger strikes can be powerful tools for peaceful resistance in our societies, especially where they have "religious" motives, biblical fasting is actually something else.

When the Christian Reformed Church began the World Hunger Sunday program in the 1970s, it was intended to heighten our collective awareness of malnutrition around the globe. The challenge given was to fast on World Hunger Sunday and then give the cost for your usual meals to hungry folks elsewhere. While the idea is noble, and I wholeheartedly endorse it, that is *not* what fasting is about, either.

WHY DID PEOPLE FAST?

In the world of Jesus' day, there were three specific reasons why people fasted.

The first was *repentance.* They fasted because they had sinned. They fasted because they had done something wrong. They fasted to say to God: I'm sorry, I'm really sorry.

I remember when my older sister first got her driver's license. Suddenly she knew how to drive. That summer we were going on a long trip together as a family. The day before we left, Jean asked if she could wash the car and get it ready for the travels. It was a nice thought, of course, but what she really wanted was a chance to drive the car.

Mom and Dad had told her often, "Make sure you check behind you when you back up. Watch out for anyone else who might be there." So after Jean got in the car and started it, stepped on the brake and slipped the gear shift into reverse, she obediently turned around and looked back to make sure there was no one behind. She let off the brake and revved the engine. As she looked back, she turned the wheel.

Crunch! She proved the law of physics: two bodies of matter cannot occupy the same place at the same time. We lived on a farm in the Minnesota countryside, and our garage was an ancient horse buggy barn with very small doors. The car could barely squeeze in and out. Jean had wrapped the left front fender around the doorjamb on the garage.

I'll never forget what she did then. She jumped out of the car crying and shouting, "I'm so sorry! I'm so sorry! I'll stay home! I won't go on vacation!"

She was saying what we all need to say sometimes: if you do something wrong, you need to make amends, and that might include giving up something significant to you.

So it is with fasting. Great King David fasted after he did his thing with Bathsheba. He was up on his palace roof one summer's evening. The day had been hot, and he wanted to catch a breeze as the sun set. Then he saw her. She was beautiful!

So he arranged to have an affair with her. He cleared her military husband from the picture in a strategic battle move. "Send Uriah in on a suicide mission," he ordered Commander Joab. The next thing you know, Bathsheba is living in the king's house, pregnant with David's child. He's the king. He can get away with it. It all belongs to him anyway, right?

But kings can stumble, and great kings can sin greatly. When God checked in with David through Nathan the Prophet, David collapsed in grief. "What have I done?" he cried and wept. "How did I get myself into this? Where did I sell my soul to turn this corner?"

That's when David fasted. He fell on the floor of his room in prayer and repentance, and he would eat no food until God resolved the matter with him. That's why people fast. They know just how deep sin sinks into their lives, and they know that without the struggles of pain in the body there is sometimes no struggle of agony in the spirit.

The Bible tells us of other fasts like that. King Ahab fasted in repentance before God after he and Jezebel stole Naboth's reputation, life, and property. The people of Nineveh fasted in repentance to God after Jonah shouted his warning through the city streets. Fasting was even built into the regular rhythm of Israel's life as a nation. There was the annual Day of Atonement, when the whole nation fasted and prayed. They had a sense that it was possible to flit through life too carelessly, without taking stock of the grit of sin that sticks to the soles of our feet, and the tether of evil that snags our hearts at inopportune moments.

Abraham Lincoln said the same thing. The year was 1863, and the Civil War ripped the nation's belly. Lincoln said this couldn't be! Who are we? What have we become as a nation? He called the people of this nation together on Thursday, April 30, to spend the entire day in fasting and prayer. In his official proclamation he said, "It is the duty of nations as well as of men to own their dependence upon the overruling power of God: to confess their sins and transgressions in humble sorrow . . . The awful calamity of civil war which now desolates the land may be but a punishment inflicted upon us for our presumptuous sins. Intoxicated with unbroken success, we have become too self-sufficient to feel the necessity, and too proud to pray to the God that made us."

The second reason people fasted in Bible times was to *remember*. When King Saul and Prince Jonathan died in battle with the Philistines, David, who took up the reigns of power, called the nation of Israel to a day of fasting because something tragic had happened. When tragedy strikes, only the careless and the cowardly and the callous are unmoved. "No man is an Island," writes John Donne. "Any man's death diminishes me, because I am involved in Mankind!"

Daniel fasted when he remembered the destruction of Jerusalem and the loss of his people's homeland. And in Jesus' day, there was an annual fast to remember the holocaust that nearly wiped out the Hebrew race when the hordes of Babylon swept down from the hills of Ephraim.

Fasting showed solidarity. Fasting declared shared involvement. Fasting said, what happened was tragic, and I will not forget the pain of it.

The third reason people fasted during Jesus' day was to *rivet attention* on God.

Earlier this week one of our daughters came to me as I was working on a letter at the computer and asked me a question about her homework. Around us other distractions raged. The television shouted the world news. Our other daughters were engaged in a noisy argument. Suddenly I realized that I couldn't concentrate. I had to pause and consciously tune out the other messages in order to focus my attention on the one who came to me for help.

So it is with our lives before God. When Queen Esther had to go to her husband, Persian King Xerxes, to plead for the life of her people, she asked her friends to fast with her. She couldn't do something like that without getting in tune with the spiritual dimensions of her soul.

In a similar incident, when Ezra was about to lead a contingent of Jews across the desert wastes to Jerusalem, they gathered food for the journey, obtained letters of legal documentation, and organized the travel groups. But when they had finished their other preparations, they fasted together for several days, riveting their attention on God, whose leading they hoped to follow.

Jesus fasted for forty days before he started his public ministry. Can you imagine that? The very son of God fasted in order to get in touch with his own father.

In Acts 13 we find Paul and Barnabas fasting and praying, and the whole congregation at Antioch with them, in order to find the future directions of the ministry God was calling them to. Fasting helps people get in touch with God.

WHAT DOES IT MEAN FOR ME TO FAST?

Let's get very specific now. Do you ever fast?

I know you do, at least in some way. What's that meal called, first thing in the morning? Breakfast? Ever think about the meaning of that word? Breakfast is the meal which *breaks* our *fast* of the night hours. So we all do fast, at least in one way. We all fast while we sleep at night.

But do you ever fast in other ways? In a purely religious way? Sounds a bit corny, doesn't it?

Why should any of us fast?

I can think of two reasons. The first is this: when I fast, I declare a religious truth. I am not merely a consumer. There's something more to me than just my appetites.

That sounds so easy to say, but in our consumer-oriented society, it has a tough feel about it. Some time ago, Brenda volunteered to drive on a school field trip. Our daughter climbed in with a few of her friends. Our car was nearly eleven years old at the time, rusted in spots, and showing more than 150,000 miles on its odometer. It wasn't as nice as it used to be, and our daughter was embarrassed to have her friends riding in her parents' old car.

That evening we talked about it together as a family. We could get a new car. After all, one of our sets of parents wanted to help us financially right then, so we could have gotten a better vehicle than that one.

But what would have been the point? Should we get a new car simply because we could? Should we buy something we want, merely because we want it?

There's nothing wrong with wealth. But the danger of our society is to say that if you can afford something you like, you deserve to have it. You *need* to buy it.

Then comes Jesus, and all he says is this: "When you fast . . ." With those words he reminds us that it takes real effort to keep from being swallowed up by our consumer-oriented society.

We desire, so we take. We want and we have the wherewithal to make it happen, so we do. We're hungry, so we eat.

But fasting stops us. It pulls us up short, because there is no greater craving than the hunger for food. Our days are organized around it—coffee breaks, lunch breaks, supper hour, snacks. When we stop eating for a while, we make a religious statement. We say there is more to us than just our appetites. There's something left of our wills. There's something bigger about our spirits. We are still masters of our flesh.

When you're addicted to drugs, you can't stop on your own. You need that next fix, that next hit, that next pill. When alcoholism grips you, you'll do anything to get another bottle.

But what about the addictions of the soul that society says are okay? What about the fads of fashion and culture that rule our shopping habits and our eating habits and our sexual habits? Can you wear less than you can afford? Can you drive a vehicle inferior to what you have the means to buy? Can you develop a relationship with someone else without jumping into bed before marriage? Can you do it?

You won't know until you've tested your soul the way that fasting tests the hunger of your body. You and I are gripped with powerful diseases of the flesh beyond which we're often willing to admit, and the medicine of fasting is one way to check out just how deep the cancer cuts.

There's a second reason why we need to fast: we fast in order to find the contours of our personalities.

Who are you? Do you know? Yes, you are your ambitions. Yes, you are your abilities. Yes, you're even your relationships.

But you are also your "nos." You and I are found, at least in part, in the nos of our lives. G. K. Chesterton put it this way: "Art and morality have this in common—they both know where to draw the lines."

When you know where to draw the lines on the picture, it begins to have beauty and meaning. When you know where to draw the lines on a building, it begins to have definition and purpose. And when you know where to draw the line in your life, you begin to have character.

The person who will stop at nothing will say yes to anything. The man who has no limits also has no identity of his own. He robs it from the victims of his cruelties. The woman who doesn't know how to say no will never be able to say yes to the things in life that matter most. And the child who isn't taught the boundaries of behavior grows up to be an adult without a conscience.

But lines are hard to draw, and character is difficult to fashion. Limits are tough to set, especially when society laughs at the pointlessness of it all.

Fasting is a spiritual discipline that takes us back to our roots, that sets us down in the company of the great ones of the past, that teaches us the mastery of God over self and helps us find our way back home. Our identity is found, at least in great measure, exactly at the points in our lives where we will say no. The yes of my life falls precisely within the limits of my no, and fasting will test those limits for me.

A few years ago, *People* magazine interviewed Dolly Parton (January 19, 1981). At one point the interviewer asked, "Where did you ever get such a strong character?"

Dolly said it came from her family and her Christian faith. "I quote the Bible real good!" she said.

What about psychiatry? asked the interviewer. So many people find the need to get counseling, especially in the stresses of show business.

"No," replied Dolly, "I don't see a psychiatrist. I fast instead."

"You what?"

"I fast."

"Is that like a diet?"

"No," said Dolly. "I do it to get in touch with God. Sometimes I'll . . . fast seven, fourteen, or twenty-one days. . . . I don't drink nothing but water and I don't ever say when I'm on a fast—Scripture says you're not supposed to."

Then she went on to say that she's never made a major decision without fasting and prayer. The interviewer was astounded, so much so that she made a point of it in the article.

But the truth of it remains. Jesus expected us to fast, and when we do, we find the contours of our souls. We find the definition of our characters. We find out who we really are before God.

Says poet Edna St. Vincent Millay:

I drank at every vine.
    The last was like the first.
I came upon no wine
    So wonderful as thirst.
I gnawed at every root,
    I ate of every plant.
I came upon no fruit
    So wonderful as want.
Feed the grape and the bean
    To the vintner and the monger;
I will lie down lean
    With my thirst and my hunger.

What does she mean? She means that there's a hungering in our souls that food can't fill, and there's a thirsting in our spirits that drink can't supply, and sometimes the only way to find out who we really are is to fast. Say no to your appetites, and yes to God.

"Do not store up for yourselves treasures on earth, where moth and rust destroy, and where thieves break in and steal. But store up for yourselves treasures in heaven, where moth and rust do not destroy, and where thieves do not break in and steal. For where your treasure is, there your heart will be also.

"The eye is the lamp of the body. If your eyes are good, your whole body will be full of light. But if your eyes are bad, your whole body will be full of darkness. If then the light within you is darkness, how great is that darkness!

"No one can serve two masters. Either he will hate the one and love the other, or he will be devoted to the one and despise the other. You cannot serve both God and Money.

"Therefore I tell you, do not worry about your life, what you will eat or drink; or about your body, what you will wear. Is not life more important than food, and the body more important than clothes? Look at the birds of the air; they do not sow or reap or store away in barns, and yet your heavenly Father feeds them. Are you not much more valuable than they? Who of you by worrying can add a single hour to his life ?

"And why do you worry about clothes? See how the lilies of the field grow. They do not labor or spin. Yet I tell you that not even Solomon in all his splendor was dressed like one of these. If that is how God clothes the grass of the field, which is here today and tomorrow is thrown into the fire, will he not much more clothe you, O you of little faith? So do not worry, saying, 'What shall we eat?' or 'What shall we drink?' or 'What shall we wear?' For the pagans run after all these things, and your heavenly Father knows that you need them. But seek first his kingdom and his righteousness, and all these things will be given to you as well. Therefore do not worry about tomorrow, for tomorrow will worry about itself. Each day has enough trouble of its own."

—Matthew 6:19–34

11
THE WORRY TEST

Monitoring Stress Tests at Heaven's Hospital

SOME YEARS AGO the most popular song around the world was Bobbie McFerrin's little diddy "Don't Worry, Be Happy." People hummed it everywhere, and radio stations of all varieties played its catchy optimistic message. No matter what happens in life, one should never worry. Just live and be happy.

Since millions and millions of people bought recordings of that song, you would think that no one would be anxious anymore. Unfortunately, even with all that airplay, Bobbie McFerrin's song failed to chase the worry warts from our souls.

One man tells of sitting next to a fellow Christian taking his first flight. The novice was obviously ill at ease, squirming in his seat, looking out the window to see if the wings were still there, gripping the armrests in a knuckle lock. Every little bump or jolt would bring a gasp and a prayer and a hand nervously fingering a rosary bead.

The experienced traveler grinned a bit and thought he might calm his seatmate's nerves with some religious psychology. "What are you so worried about?" he asked. "Didn't Jesus say in the Bible, 'I am with you always, even to the ends of the earth?'"

"No!" the other passenger shouted. "You've got it wrong! Jesus said, '*Lo*, I am with you always.' I'm not sure what happens when you get way up here!"

WORRY IS PART OF LIFE

High or low, worry is part of human life. Jesus understands that. In fact, the Bible seems to indicate that Jesus worried at times right along with the rest of us. In John 12, we read of Jesus' entry into Jerusalem at the start of the week that would bring his death. The crowds surrounded him, and he was well aware of the troubles that would come in the next few days. When he arrives at the Temple square to pray, he shouts a note of worry to the skies. "Now my heart is troubled!" he says. The word he uses, as it comes to us in the Greek text, is one that echoes our fears. It means agitated, unsettled, anxious, frightened, or disturbed.

Jesus sounds like one of us, doesn't he? He worried too.

But when you think about that, should it be so unusual? Jesus was fully human, just as we are. He was as normal, during his times on earth, as the person sitting next to him. The only difference, according to the Bible, is that in his worries, Jesus never stepped across the line that would have led him to sin.

Worry is a part of human life. Do you know anyone who never worries? Only a machine can't worry. Only a robot never gets anxious.

A newspaper columnist once wrote about the fears of a young fellow on the way to his first day at school: "My name is Donald, and I don't know anything! I have new underwear, a new sweater, a loose tooth, and I didn't sleep well last night; I worried. What if the school bus jerks after I get on, and I lose my balance and my pants rip and everyone laughs? What if a bell rings and a man yells, 'Where do you belong?' and I don't know? What if the thermos lid on my soup is on too tight, and when I try to open it, it breaks? What if I splash water on my name tag, and my name disappears, and no one will know who I am? What if they send us out to play, and all the swings are taken?"

Though she writes about a child, that columnist echoes our own everyday fears.

We all worry. It's part of life. A reporter once asked G. K. Chesterton, "If you were a preacher and you had only one sermon to give, what would it be about?"

Chesterton didn't think twice. He said, "I'd preach about worry." He knew what it was to be human. Worry is a part of life, and something that drives a lot of our actions. Jesus knows that. That's why he focused on worry for such a large portion of the Sermon on the Mount.

WE WORRY ABOUT THINGS THAT MATTER TO US

Jesus' list of worries comes from the morning newspaper. We worry about food, he says, and about our health. We worry about the kinds of clothes we wear: Are they in fashion? Will people notice me? Do they respect me or laugh behind my back?

More than that, says Jesus, we worry about money. We worry about mortgages and interest rates. We worry about pensions and taxes.

Jesus knows us pretty well. Everything on his list of worries *is* important, isn't it? We *should* be concerned about our health. It *is* important to pay our bills. In fact, we get upset with people who don't pay their bills. When we sing along with Bobby McFerrin's "Don't Worry, Be Happy," we mumble through the part that says, "Landlord say your rent is late / He might have to litigate." We don't want too many of Bobby McFerrin's carefree friends leasing our properties and paying no rent or living next door to us on welfare.

Jesus can't be telling us to be careless about ourselves and our things. After all, he also teaches us to pray, "Father, give us today our daily bread." He expects us to be concerned about things that are close to us and a common part of life.

And that's what we worry about, isn't it? We worry about the things that are close to us, the things that are constantly with us, and the things that we carry around with us day after day. We worry about the things that have the most immediate value to us.

Maybe that's really the point of what Jesus is trying to say. Our worries are essentially the test of our values. We worry about things that are the most important to us in life.

That's why Jesus encourages us to take the Worry Test. What are you most anxious about? What troubles you the most? What keeps you awake at night or disturbs your thoughts most often during the day?

When we take the test, we find out where our hearts are. The worry test teaches us the schedule of values in our lives.

It's like the story someone told of two men on a cross-country bike trip. They're traveling together on a tandem bike. For the first few miles the land is level and they pump along with energy and style, enjoying this teamwork. But then the road begins to rise, and they find themselves fighting a steep climb. Panting and puffing, they slowly work their way to the top.

Finally they reach the summit and stop to catch their breaths. "Whew!" says one, wiping the sweat off his face, "that was some hard climb!"

"Yeah!" says the other, "and if I hadn't kept the brake on, we probably would have slid back to the bottom!"

That's the Worry Test in action, isn't it? The one fellow had his mind on the heights. He was going to make it to the top if it took all of his energies and strength. Meanwhile his partner has his mind on the bottom. He's worried about sliding back down the hill. They're both doing the same thing, riding the same bike on the same road up the same hill, but their values are at different places. Their worries set them apart.

So it is with us. We all worry, but our worries surround the things that we value most in life. List the concerns that bother you the most. When you read your list over, you'll find your heart: "For where your treasure is, there your heart will be also" (Matthew 6:21).

WHAT DO YOU WORRY ABOUT?

So the challenge of Jesus is not to stop worrying altogether. To be human is to have worries and frets and cares. We are affected by life. The issue, according to Jesus, is to change our goals and values and treasure so that, in the end, our worries will take on a more godly character. "Seek first the Kingdom of God and his righteousness," says Jesus, "and all these things that you need will come to you as well."

During his days in the Siberian labor camps, Alexander Solzhenitsyn had lost his family. His days stretched out in endless, backbreaking efforts. Then the doctors told him he had cancer. There was no cure. He would die soon.

The next day, he could barely get out of his bunk. His heart was gone. His mind was numb. He had no energy as he left to join the others in the dawn work patrol. "What's the use?" he asked himself.

Solzhenitsyn writes that when he got to the rock quarries, he dropped his shovel, sat down, resting his head on his tired, folded arms. He knew the guards would see him soon, but he didn't care. He hoped that they would shoot him. Then, at least, the pain would be over and the worries gone.

"Just then," he writes, "I felt someone standing near me. I looked up, and there was an old man. I'd never seen him before. I don't remember ever seeing him again. But he knelt over me, and he took a stick, and he drew a cross on the ground in front of me.

"That cross," he said, "made me see things in a new way. There's a Power in this universe that is bigger than any empire or any government. There's a God who experiences our pain and who dies our death and who came back from the tombs. There's a God who gives life meaning, who is life itself. That's what really matters here. That's why we exist. That's why Jesus came to earth for us."

Solzhenitsyn says that he sat there thinking about it all for a few more minutes. Then he stood up, picked up his shovel, and went back to work. Things wouldn't change around him for over a year, but inside he was a new person.

That incident put Solzhenitsyn's worries in their place. They didn't vanish or disappear suddenly. Instead, they were caught up into a larger perspective of concern. How could he share the life of the Master? How could his days be a reflection of God's Kingdom, God's Power, and God's Glory?

That's where Jesus is leading us, as well. "Seek first the Kingdom of God and his righteousness," he says.

But that is a hard lesson to learn. We are so good at taking control of our lives. We are very good at trying to play God, to the point that we don't want him to remind us of the real structures of life.

Some years ago, when Dick Shepard was the vicar of an Anglican parish in London, he had a dream. It was vivid and stayed with him after he awoke. His life was exceptionally busy in those days. He was constantly trying to meet the demands of the many people under his care in ministry.

One day he felt himself coming down with the flu. But he couldn't afford to get sick. He didn't have the time. There were too many things to do. There were sermons to write and classes to prepare and meetings to chair and people to visit. His congregation needed him. His family needed him. Even God needed him. He just couldn't afford to get sick right now.

That night he had his terrible nightmare. He dreamed that he was standing in heaven near to God's throne. An angelic telegram arrived, and the messenger handed the envelope to God. God tore it open and read these horrifying words: "Dick Shepard is about to be ill."

Then, said Rev. Shepard, God began to wring his hands. A worried look clouded God's face, and he began to mumble, "Oh, no! Dick Shepard is about to be ill! Whatever shall I do? Whatever shall I do?"

When Pastor Shepard woke up in the morning, he had a good laugh. He decided that God could probably manage somehow without him, and he stopped living as if all the world depended on him.

That's the lesson that Jesus wants to teach us. It will change our values and redefine our goals and point us toward new treasures. "Your heavenly father knows," says Jesus. And that's enough.

Fred Craddock reminds us of that in a story about a sermon of his that took on a life of its own. The sermon was titled "Doxology," and he had preached it a number of times; enough so that it gained quite a reputation among his family and friends. The message of "Doxology" was all about the meaning of life and the reason why we exist. It said that the ultimate goal of our time on earth is to bring glory to God, no matter what the circumstances. Fred says that that sermon led to one of the most beautiful experiences of his life.

"I was on the phone," he writes. "My oldest brother had just died. Heart attack. When stunned and hurt, I get real busy to avoid thinking.

"Call the wife. Get the kids out of school. Arrange for a colleague to take my classes. Cancel a speaking engagement.

"And, oh yes, stop the milk, the paper, the mail; have someone feed the dog . . .

"All night we drove across two states, eyes pasted against the windshield. Conversation was spasmodic, consisting of taking turns asking the same question over and over.

"When we drew near the town and the house, I searched my mind for a word to speak to the widow. He was my brother, but he was her husband. I was still searching when we pulled into the driveway. She came out to meet us and as I opened the car door, still without that word, she broke the silence with, 'I hope you brought 'Doxology!'

"'Doxology'?" writes Fred. "No, I hadn't even thought of [that sermon] since the phone call. But the truth is now clear: if we ever lose our Doxology, we might as well be dead."

Isn't that true? We'll never stop worrying. We'll never still our anxious hearts. But when we take the Worry Test, and when we find out where our treasures really lie, and when we learn to sing the Doxology in all circumstances of life, then Jesus' words will have come home in us.

"Do not judge, or you too will be judged. For in the same way you judge others, you will be judged, and with the measure you use, it will be measured to you.

"Why do you look at the speck of sawdust in your brother's eye and pay no attention to the plank in your own eye? How can you say to your brother, 'Let me take the speck out of your eye,' when all the time there is a plank in your own eye? You hypocrite, first take the plank out of your own eye, and then you will see clearly to remove the speck from your brother's eye.

"Do not give dogs what is sacred; do not throw your pearls to pigs. If you do, they may trample them under their feet, and then turn and tear you to pieces."

—Matthew 7:1–6

12
A NEW PAIR OF GLASSES

Can You Really Read the Bottom Line?

NORWEGIAN PLAYWRIGHT HENRIK IBSEN was traveling in Rome when he noticed a crowd of people gathered around a large red poster. They were talking excitedly among themselves about the message it announced, so he reached into his coat pocket for his eyeglasses, only to realize that he had left them back at his hotel room.

He turned to the man standing next to him and said, "Signore, could you please tell me what the sign says? I've forgotten my glasses."

"Sorry, signore," said the other fellow, with a knowing look in his eyes, "But I don't know how to read either."

Glasses are a necessary evil for many of us. I can't get along without glasses at all. If I take mine off, I can't see clearly anything that is more than seven inches away.

Our youngest daughter used to think that I couldn't have any bad dreams at night because I always slept without my glasses. She thought that I couldn't see any of the monsters who might have otherwise chased me through the nightmare worlds of my subconscious.

Of course, if that were the case, I wouldn't be able to have any good dreams either. Songwriter Kurt Weill said something like that when he reflected on his fortunes in marriage. He had very bad eyesight and wore thick glasses.

One day, when he was out in a rowboat with singer Lotte Lenya, she accidentally knocked his glasses into the water (at least that's the way *she* tells the story). He was practically blind after that, so she had to row the boat ashore and lead him around for the rest of the day.

It was later on that same day that Kurt asked Lotte to marry him. When she said, "Yes!" they decided to tie the knot as quickly as possible. Kurt didn't even have an opportunity to get a new pair of glasses made before their wedding day.

Lotte was never considered very beautiful, and some time after their marriage she turned to Kurt, now wearing his new eyeglasses, even thicker than the ones before, and she said to him, "Do you think you would have married me if you were wearing glasses at the time?"

How would you answer a question like that with grace and integrity?

We would all like to think that we would say, "Sure! Of course! I love you for what you are inside, not just for how you look!"

But are we really like that? Is that actually the way we think? If we are honest, appearances do mean a lot to us.

Jesus knows that. He knows the way that we look at each other, and he knows the judgments that we make about each other. That's why, in Matthew 7:1–6, he tells us to get a new pair of glasses. Not just the kind that sit on our noses, but the kind that fit on our hearts and minds, the kind that help us see people in a new way.

Dr. Karl Menninger once said, "Attitudes are more important than facts." That's essentially what Jesus says here about the new pair of glasses that each of us needs. We need glasses that will change our attitudes about each other. We need the ability to alter our perceptions. We need a change in heart that will allow us to believe in people, encourage them, and to build others up instead of cutting them down.

THESE GLASSES HELP US SEE PEOPLE AS GOD SEES

They are the kind of glasses, says Jesus in verses 1–2, that help us see other people as God sees them, to see the inside better than the outside.

When I was young my friends and I used to love the magazine *Popular Mechanics*. It was full of neat projects and all the latest gadgets and gizmos. At the back of each issue there was a section of advertisements, one of which intrigued us immensely. If we had enough money and if we sent it to the right address, we would receive by mail a pair of x-ray glasses! According to the ads, they would allow you to see right inside of people. You could get past all the clothing. You could get right under the skin. You could see the muscles and the skeleton and all of the internal organs.

Well, we never had the money. Besides, none of us really dared to send for anything like that. What would we say to our parents when the package came in the mail?

The Bible, however, always talks about God as having glasses just like that. "You judge by outward appearances," Jesus says, "but God looks at the heart." He's not impressed with all the beauty and power and strength that we put so much stock in.

Nor is he as critical as we are. That's the striking thing in what Jesus says. Often we are so used to thinking about the wrath and judgment and anger of God that we overlook this idea. Yet the whole point of what Jesus says in verse 2 is that in the Christian community, God chooses to see the good in us. He chooses to see us through eyes of love. He has decided to look toward us favorably.

That can be a powerful influence in a person's life. One writer tells of attending a business conference where awards were being given for outstanding achievements during the past fiscal year. A woman came to the podium to receive the company's top honor. As she clutched the trophy in her hands, she beamed at the crowd of over three thousand people. Yet, in that moment of triumph, she had eyes for only one person. She looked directly at her supervisor, a woman named Joan.

The award-winner told of the difficult times she had gone through only a few years earlier. She had experienced personal problems, and, for a time, her work had suffered. Some people turned away from her, counting it a liability to be seen with her. Others wrote her off as a loser in the company.

The worst part of it all was that she felt like a loser. She had stopped at Joan's desk several times with a letter of resignation in her hand. She was a failure. She wanted to quit.

But Joan said, "Let's just wait a little bit longer." And Joan said, "Give it one more try." And Joan said, "I never would have hired you if I didn't think you could handle it."

The award-winner's voice broke. Tears streamed down her cheeks. Softly, she said, "Joan believed in me more than I believed in myself!"

Isn't that the message of the Gospel? Isn't that the story of the Bible? That God believed in us while we were still sinners, while we were still failures, while we were at the point in our lives that we couldn't seem to make it on our own? "You were dead in your trespasses and sins," writes the Apostle Paul, "but God made you alive in Jesus Christ" (Col. 2:13). "God so loved the world," Jesus says in John 3:16, " . . . that whoever believes in him shall not perish but have eternal life." The God who loves us in that way is not a God who evaluates us harshly. He knows us inside and out, but he chooses to call us friends.

You know the story of the woman who went to the portrait artist. She was a rather difficult person to please. A number of other painters had failed when she commissioned them to capture her likeness on canvas. "Young man," she told the painter sternly, "I want you to do me justice."

He looked her up and down, and finally said, "Madam, what you need is mercy."

That's Jesus' point in Matthew 7:2. We want to deal in justice. We'll find fault in others. We'll be keen about their failures and mistakes and sins. We will do them justice.

But that's not how God handles you. That's not what your religion is all about. If you want to handle others only with justice, then, in the end, it will be justice that you yourself receive, not mercy.

Get God's glasses, and learn to see people the way that he sees them: with mercy, with love, with respect.

THESE GLASSES HELP US SEE PEOPLE AS THEY REALLY ARE

There is a second thing that Jesus' glasses help us do, and that is to see people as they really are.

One mother tells of a difficult time she was having with her young daughter. They seemed to be going through a testing period, and the girl was doing something wrong nearly every day. The mother would scold and punish and raise her voice. Some days were better than others, but it was a tough time for both of them.

One day things went pretty well. The little girl tried especially hard to be good and to please her mother. That night, after she tucked her daughter in bed, the mother says that she was heading down the stairs when she heard her daughter sobbing into her pillow. Alarmed, the mother went back to the bedroom and asked what was wrong. Her daughter burst into tears and cried out to her mother, "Haven't I been a little bit good today?"

The mother says, "That question went through me like a knife. I was so quick to correct her when she did wrong, but when she was good, I didn't even notice."

That's what Jesus is talking about in Matthew 7:3–5. We so often see only what we want to see. And what we want to see is the worst in other people. When we look only for the bad, we belittle who people really are.

Some years ago a psychologist named Aldrich published a fascinating article. He had worked for years in social services. Most of his time was spent with teenagers who had been arrested for shoplifting and other kinds of theft. His job was to interview them and find out how they had gotten into this practice. Aldrich also talked with the parents, attempting to discover how they had handled the problem from the first time they knew about it.

Over the years, he kept a record of all his interviews. Gradually they seemed to separate into two lists. One list contained the names of those who became repeat offenders and showed up in the criminal justice system again and again. The other listed those who were with him one time and then stayed straight.

He concluded there were basically two ways parents responded to the first shoplifting incident. One group of parents confronted their child this way: "Now we know what you are. You're a thief! We'll be watching you now, buddy! Don't think you can get away with this again!"

The other group of parents said something like this: "Tom, that wasn't like you at all. We'll have to go back to the store and clear this thing up, but then it's done with, okay? What you did was wrong. You know that it was wrong. But we're sure you won't do it again."

Aldrich discovered that the parents who assumed the worst usually got the worst, and the parents who assumed the best most often got the best.

It's interesting that Jesus talks about something foreign getting into our eyes, something alien that doesn't really belong there. It's not part of our essence. Yet, he says, it's the very thing that we use to evaluate other people. When you look at your brother, what do you see? Do you see the speck in his eye? Do you see only the little thing that's wrong, the little thing that's abnormal, the little thing that isn't really true to character? Then, do you base your actions toward him on that one thing? Can you think only of how awful he is, and how terrible his condition is, and how badly you need to correct him?

Mark Twain used to say, "You can't depend on your eyes when your imagination is out of focus." That is Jesus' point as well. Sometimes our imaginations about others get so far out of focus that our eyes can't see clearly anymore.

How do you see others around you? What are your first thoughts about them? There was an advertisement by the Atlantic-Richfield Company some years ago. It went like this: "We must teach our children not only *what* to see, but also *how* to see." Jesus says that that is a lesson we all have to learn.

When we do, we begin to see people as they really are: good, right, and noble. Each person has flaws, failures and imperfections, but that's not the essence of one's character when God is at work in one's life.

THESE GLASSES HELP US SEE PEOPLE AS THEY CAN BECOME

The glasses Jesus wants us to put on help us to see others around us as God sees them, and they help us to see others as they really are. There's a third thing they do for us: they help us see people as they can become.

That is really the significance of the strange little statement Jesus makes in Matthew 7:6: "Do not give dogs what is sacred; do not throw your pearls to pigs. If you do, they may trample them under their feet and then turn and tear you to pieces."

There have been a number of interpretations of this particular verse. Usually Bible teachers reflect on how we are supposed to treat people in the church one way and people outside the church another way. The *Didache*, an early training manual of the Syrian Christian community written around A.D. 100, uses this statement as a warning to keep some people away from the communion table. Other interpretations say that Jesus adds it to the rest of what he says here to make sure that we don't get carried away with our good thoughts about those around us. We have to be practical, they say. We can't just let others walk all over us.

There is, however, another interpretation of this little proverb. In our English Bibles, the words are translated as commands: "Don't do this! Don't give the holy things to dogs! Don't give pearls to pigs!" But actually, in the original Greek, there is no command at all. The statements are more descriptive than imperative. They can be read like this: "You don't do this, do you? You wouldn't give holy things to dogs, would you? You wouldn't throw your jewelry to the pigs, would you?"

The implication of reading Jesus' proverb like that is obvious. The way you see people is the way that they become for you. The way you treat people determines what they will be.

Robert Rosenthal, a Harvard University psychologist, and Lenore Jacobson, a San Francisco school principal, once did a study that affirmed this. They gave a learning ability test to all the students in one school, kindergarten through fifth grade. Then, without taking a look at the scores, they randomly selected five names from each class.

The next September, when the new school term began, they casually dropped the hint to the new teachers that these particular students were exceptional. They were the bright ones. They were likely to push on ahead of the rest.

And they did. At the end of the school year, the learning ability tests were given again. The five students from each class identified in the previous year as gifted were now all at the top of their classes. Some had gained nearly thirty points on IQ tests. The teachers in each grade were consistent in their praise. These students were indeed the happiest, the most curious, the most affectionate children in their classes. Without a doubt, the teachers said, these children would be successful in later life. They had it in them.

Said the German poet Goethe, "Treat a man as he appears to be and you make him worse. But treat a man as if he already were what he potentially could be, and you make him what he should be."

Jesus' thought is much the same. You don't throw your treasures to dogs. You expect the worst from dogs, and you get it. You don't hand your jewelry over to the pigs. You know what they will do with it. The same goes for people. When you treat people as if they were dogs, and when you expect people to be pigs, why are you surprised if they become what you think?

Look at people with your new pair of glasses. See those around you with the potential of their souls; see what they become.

Albert Einstein was four years old before he could speak and seven years old before he could read. Sir Isaac Newton did poorly in elementary school. A newspaper editor once fired Walt Disney, saying, "He has no good ideas." The great Russian author Leo Tolstoy flunked out of college. Wernher von Braun, the scientist who first fired rockets into outer space, failed his ninth grade algebra class. And when Franz Joseph Haydn was trying to teach a new pupil about music, he called the young man "slow and plodding, with no apparent talent." That young student was Ludwig von Beethoven.

But with each of these people one other person—a teacher, a parent, a friend—said to him, "You can do it. You've got it in you. Give it another try." And the dogs become scientists. The pigs became artists. The losers blossomed. All because someone had the grace of God to see them as they could become.

In 1939 trainloads of Jewish children streamed into Sweden. Parents were trying to get them out of Germany. Boys and girls came off the cars, some only three or four years old. They had nothing with them except a tag around their necks that gave their names, their home towns, and their ages. That's all they had in life.

The Swedes had agreed to take the children in "for the duration of the war." Yet when they parceled the children out, there were more of the little ones than there were welcoming homes. They pleaded with other families to open their homes. One host who came on the scene rather late was Johan Eriksson. He was a widower, middle-aged, and alone in his house. Not the best candidate to do this kind of thing, but little Rolf needed a place to stay, so the authorities put him in Johan's care.

Rolf was starving. He was frightened so badly that he wouldn't talk at all. Every time there was a noise at the door, he would run into a closet and pull something over his head.

It took years before Rolf put on any weight, and longer still before the hint of a smile turned his lips. At the end of the war, they never found Rolf's parents. Hitler's ovens had taken care of that.

Rolf eventually went away to Stockholm. He tried his hand at business, but things didn't work out for him. Rolf's boss said, "His mind just snapped one day." Local authorities wanted to put him in a mental institution.

But Johan was there. He was an old man now. Still, he took Rolf home with him again to the little city of Amal. For years Johan nursed Rolf back to health.

Rolf finally got better. He married a wonderful woman. He established a successful business and became wealthy. It was only because of Johan, the big Swede who took in a nobody, loved him back to life, gave him an identity, and hugged away his fears.

When the doctors called Johan's children home for a final parting in his dying days, Rolf was the first to arrive.

Johan was a Christian. He read the Sermon on the Mount. And he put on that new pair of glasses Jesus talks about. He saw little Rolf as God saw him. He saw little Rolf as he really was inside. And he saw little Rolf as he could become. The day that Rolf met Johan was the day that Rolf began to live.

Have you put on your new pair of glasses?

"Ask and it will be given to you; seek and you will find; knock and the door will be opened to you. For everyone who asks receives; he who seeks finds; and to him who knocks, the door will be opened.

"Which of you, if his son asks for bread, will give him a stone? Or if he asks for a fish, will give him a snake? If you, then, though you are evil, know how to give good gifts to your children, how much more will your Father in heaven give good gifts to those who ask him! So in everything, do to others what you would have them do to you, for this sums up the Law and the Prophets."

—Matthew 7:7–12

13
HOW WELL DO YOU KNOW YOUR FATHER?

Learning the Cosmic Lesson on Family Values

HOW WELL DO YOU know your father? Have you ever thought about that? If he is no longer living, how well did you know him as you grew up?

I thought about that once when I saw a *Peanuts* cartoon. Charlie Brown is talking to his pal Linus, leaning on a brick fence and describing his relationship with his Dad. "My Dad likes me to come down to the barber shop and wait for him," he says. "No matter how busy he is, even if the shop is full of customers, he always stops and says 'Hi!' to me. I sit here on the bench until six o'clock, when he's through, and then we ride home together."

The next frame shows Charlie Brown deep in thought, and then, in the final scene, he shows a bright face and says, "It really doesn't take much to make my dad happy!"

Good for Charlie Brown and his dad! But sometimes fathers are more mysterious than that. Some time ago researchers at Cornell University studied family behavior across North America. The study found that the average father spends 37.7 seconds alone with each child each day, about one-third of one minute per day. Sometimes it seems that all we know about our fathers comes through observing them from a distance.

One Jewish boy in Europe grew up with a profound sense of admiration for his father. His father was very religious. The family went to services at the synagogue each week. They practiced Jewish acts of devotion in their home, and his father took a leadership role in the Jewish religious community.

Then they moved to a new town. There most of the leading businessmen belonged to the local Lutheran church. So, one day, the father announced to the family that they were all going to abandon their Jewish traditions and be baptized as members of the Lutheran church.

The boy was stunned. "Why?" he asked his dad. "Why would we do something like that?"

His father shattered him with the answer. It had nothing to do with spiritual convictions. It wasn't a sudden inspiration from God, or even a sense of disappointment with the Jewish faith. His father told him that it would be good for business. That's why they would become Christians.

The boy never recovered from the tremendous doubts that shook him that day, or the intense bitterness he felt over his father's sudden declarations. When he left home, he went to England to study. There, at the British Museum, he read and thought and wrote. Eventually he published a book that described religion as the "opiate of the masses." Everything in life, he wrote, ultimately came down to economics. The bottom line is money. The title on his manuscript said it all: *Das Kapital*.

The boy's name, of course, was Karl Marx. Today we know him as the man who developed modern atheistic communism. And it all started with his father.

What we see in our fathers has a profound impact on the way we live. It is that way, as well, in our relationship with God. That's why when Jesus teaches his disciples about prayer and the values of life, he begins by asking the question, How well do you know your Father?

You see, if we don't believe that God is a good father to us, we will never begin to pray. It is that simple. In the New Testament letter to the Hebrew Christians we read, "Anyone who comes to [God] must believe that he exists, and that he rewards those who earnestly seek him"

(Hebrews 11:6). In other words, prayer begins when we know that God cares about us like a good father would.

The late playwright Channing Pollack knew that. He used to tell a devastating tale of something that happened to him as a young boy. His parents took him along to a party at a magnificent house on a grand estate. The people who lived there and hosted the party had a young daughter about his age, so the two of them played together.

When they ran out of ideas for games, young Channing said, "Let's hide behind this curtain and maybe no one will know we're here!"

The girl never hesitated in her forlorn answer. She said, "Maybe no one will care."

Can you imagine that? A young child says about her own parents maybe no one will care. Maybe no one will ever come to check on us. Maybe they will all forget about us, and we'll stand there till we die.

Yet think of it: if there is ever any reason why people don't pray, it's because somewhere along the line they have begun to feel that way. Maybe God doesn't care. Maybe God has forgotten about me. Maybe there's no heavenly Father at all.

Luke's Gospel adds a little story to explain what Jesus means when he talks about trusting God to care about us like a good father.

You're in your bed late one night and suddenly you hear pounding at your door, and someone calling to you. Since your whole family is gathered around you in the sleeping quarters at the far end of your house, everyone is disturbed by the noise.

Why would anyone be out there so late at night? Well, in the heat of Palestinian summer, nobody travels very far during the day. Your friend is on a journey, and he traveled after sundown in the cool of the evening. Now he has finally arrived at your village.

That's why you roll away from your wife, and you try not to step on the kids, and you grab a little lamp, lighting the wick from the smoldering ashes of the cooking fire. Then you move back the sticks that keep the cattle out in the courtyard of your house. Of course, they all start to moo and bellow and grunt, the way livestock does when disturbed at night. All the while your friend is out there at the main door of your house calling for you and knocking incessantly.

Finally you get to him. You have to spend fifteen minutes out there in the street going through a whole series of greetings so as not to offend your friend.

You then retrace your steps, guiding him at your side, disturbing the noisy cattle again, passing through the gate into your eating and sleeping quarters, and treading carefully among your yawning children who are now stretching and rubbing their eyes.

Your wife is up. She knows what she's supposed to do. She says to you, "Honey, we don't have any bread."

Palestinian hospitality demands that you sit down together over a meal with a recently arrived guest, no matter what the hour, no matter what you were doing. No traveler ever comes to a home or an inn without a meal being set on the table immediately.

And since in first-century Palestine, there is no cutlery for eating, you can't get by without bread. Bread is used to dip the broth from the pot or to pick up the vegetables from the soup.

So the late night bothering has to start all over again. Only this time you are at the door of another friend's house down the street. You know what your friend is going through, there at the far end of his house, as you scratch at the door. You can hear the animals snorting and rolling inside. You can hear the children tossing and turning at the disturbance. You know he's not very pleased when he yells at you from the distance, "What's the matter out there? Don't you know how late it is? What do you want?"

You apologize profusely, but you don't go away. You keep banging, and in fits and starts relate the story of what is happening at your house. You know that your friend is thinking to himself, "Not now! We're settled for the night. We're trying to get some sleep. Come back in the morning!"

Still, you know that your friend will get up. He'll disturb all the children. He'll light the lamp and push back the sticks into the cattle courtyard. He'll grab some leftover bread and stumble through the livestock and probably even step in the manure. But he will meet you at the door, and he will give you what you want.

Why? Because the honor of the village is at stake when a traveler comes to town. Everyone will do what they can to meet the needs of hospitality.

When Jesus tells that story to his disciples in Luke 11, he helps them understand the character of their Father. Just as they know where to find the bread at night, so they can count on their Father in heaven to deliver the goods that are needed in their relationships that matter.

In fact, Jesus will sometimes use the Aramaic term *abba* for Father. *Abba* means daddy. The children in the marketplace shout it as they tug on their fathers' robes to get his attention: "Abba! Abba! Abba!"

That is the sense of what Jesus tells us concerning going to God in prayer. Daddies can fix anything that really needs fixing. Daddies are always there for us. Nothing means more to daddies than our cares and concerns. And God is our daddy in that sense.

Phil Moran tells of his early years of marriage, when four children were born to them almost in successive years. Sometimes he wondered how the house could be so busy—the endless noise, the dirty diapers, the toys scattered everywhere.

The only time he could be alone for a few minutes, in order to think or just have some peace, was when he took a shower. He remembers that even there he was disturbed at times. Once his little daughter came banging on the door, calling for him. He shouted back at her from the shower with a great voice of authority, "Can I have my privacy please?"

The knocking stopped for just the briefest moment. As he breathed a sigh of relief the tiny voice returned, "Daddy, where's your privacy? I can't find it!"

In Jesus' terms, God is a Father who gives up his privacy for us. He is never too busy to hear the things we want to tell him. He is never too occupied to listen to our cares and concerns. He is never too frustrated to spend time building his relationship with us. And that is the beginning of our feeble attempts at prayer.

Sometimes, of course, we forget that. Sometimes we are looking for the wrong things in prayer and lose sight of Jesus' teachings.

A friend told me about a Hollywood production company that was filming on location in northern California. The action in the movie was to take place on a deserted stretch of highway, but the script called for an isolated service station in one small scene.

Construction crews were sent to build the service station. It looked real enough until someone tried to pump gas. The buildings themselves were merely fronts with nothing behind. Yet from the highway everything looked authentic.

In fact, every now and again a car would actually pull in and hope for a fill. Between scenes, some of the crew members would play that out. They put on greasy coveralls and stood next to the pumps. An unsuspecting motorist would get the full treatment—nozzle in the tank, windshield washed, oil checked. Then came the surprise. The attendant would say that the service station was running a special just for today, and there was no charge for the gas.

One motorist after another drove away with a big smile. But thirty miles down the road the car sputtered to a halt, fuel gauge on empty.

My friend told me that story made him think about prayer. He said that he used to pray, but then he stopped. He always felt that prayer was a bit like pulling into that service station on the movie set. It made him feel good. It promised that things would be better, that life would be grand, and that he was getting a great deal. As he moved on, however, his requests weren't always answered, and his religion ran out of gas. Now he doesn't pray any more.

There are more of us that feel like him. We used to pray, but then we didn't seem to get what we wanted from God, so we stopped praying. It doesn't seem to make much difference in our lives anyway.

It's like the cartoon where a young boy is getting ready for bed and his mom wants him to say his prayers. He looks up at her and shakes his head. "Uncle Jim still doesn't have a job," he tells her. "Sis still doesn't have a date for the prom, and Grandma still isn't getting any better. I'm tired of praying for this family and not getting any results!"

Like him, we want to get results. We want to tap into heaven's resources. We want God to do something for us: change our lives. Change our circumstances. Change our fortunes.

Sometimes we see prayer as heaven's toll-free number: Call this number today! One of our operators is standing by to take your order! A child kneels at her bedside and shouts, "I'm gonna say my prayers now; does anybody want anything?" One wit has even described prayer this way: "It's when we put all our begs in one ask-it!"

Yet when Jesus talks to his disciples about prayer, the emphasis is not merely on getting anything we want from God. It is more about deepening our relationship with him. It has the sense of knowing that one is cared for, and the notion of turning your face toward home.

Good fathers don't give their children everything they ask for. That would never help them grow properly in life. Yet what a child needs most, a conscientious parent will always have in supply: the encouragement of worth, the confidence of belonging, and the knowledge that someone truly cares. If you really need those things in life, you know where to find them. You also know that whenever you knock on that door, your Father will be there for you.

The proof is not so much in what I say as it is in Jesus' own experience. If there were ever anyone in this world who knew God, it was Jesus. He is the one who says that these things are so.

I'm no great expert in prayer. I fail as often as anyone else. There have been many times in the past when I have been as far from prayer as Karl Marx. What brought me back to God? What gave me confidence to call him Father? How did I dare cry out again to heaven and shout the word of the child's heart, "*Abba!* Daddy!"?

In the end it was always the encouragement of Jesus. Bang at the door of heaven, says Jesus. Your Father knows what you need, and his relationship with you means more than anything else to him in the whole world. You can count on him. Maybe he won't do for you everything that you want; what father in his right mind would? Yet that isn't why you love your father in the first place. You love him because he truly loves you. You love him because he cares about you. You love him because he is willing even to give up his precious privacy for you.

That's why you pray. That's why Jesus prayed. That's why prayer is so important to us, not just for what we can get out of it but for what it means to our very souls, our very identities.

When Rembrandt sketched his famous picture of the story of the Prodigal Son returning to his Father, the single most impressive part of the drawing is this: the face on the shoulders of the son is Rembrandt's own face.

Think of the tale behind that picture. Here is a son who got whatever he wanted from his father: wealth, privileges, and freedom. Yet when he lived with that for a time, he found that it wasn't really what he needed in life. It wasn't the presents that made the difference, nor the fact that his father said yes to all he asked.

What he really needed was a relationship with his father. These other things only meant that his father cared enough about him to give up his own rights and privileges, his own comforts and concerns. His father was willing to throw everything else to the wind, if that is what it took to show his boy how much he loved him.

In that sense, our heavenly Father did the same thing for us. The apostle Paul said that God did not even spare his own son, but gave him up freely for us (Romans 8:32). That is why Rembrandt drew his own face on the shoulders of the Prodigal Son. The scene shows the young man falling into the arms of his father.

For us, that is where prayer begins.

An old legend tells the story of a father and son who were traveling together. As they came to the edge of a forest there were bushes loaded with luscious berries. The son begged the father to stop for a while and pick berries.

Although the father was anxious to be on his way, he saw the desire in his son's eyes and agreed to do what the lad so badly wanted. They searched the bushes together for the biggest, plumpest, juiciest berries.

Finally, the father knew that it was time to move on. He simply could not delay any longer. "Son," he said, "we cannot stay here all day. We must continue our journey."

The boy was not ready to go. He begged and pleaded and whined. He got angry and accused his father of not loving him. What could the father do?

The father settled the matter in this way. He said to his son, "You may pick berries for a while longer, but I must begin to go down the road. I will travel slowly, and you will be able to catch up. Be sure that you are able to find me. While you work, call out to me, 'Father! Father!' I will answer you. As long as you hear my voice you will know where I am. But as soon as you can no longer hear me, know that you are lost, and run with all your strength, calling out my name."

That's a good picture of us, isn't it? Do you still call out for your Father? Do you know where to find him? How well do you know your Father?

In the words of the old hymn by Annie Johnson Flint, "He Giveth More Grace":

> When we have exhausted our store of endurance,
> When our strength has failed 'ere the day is half done,
> When we reach the end of our hoarded resources,
> Our Father's full giving is only begun.
> His love has no limit, his grace has no measure,
> His pow'r has no boundaries known unto men;
> For out of his infinite riches in Jesus
> He giveth, and giveth, and giveth again!

That's what Jesus says, too.

"Enter through the narrow gate. For wide is the gate and broad is the road that leads to destruction, and many enter through it. But small is the gate and narrow the road that leads to life, and only a few find it."

—Matthew 7:13–14

14
CATCHING THE WRONG BUS

Check Your Ticket Before You Travel Too Far

HARRY EMERSON FOSDICK once reported a strange event. A man bought a Greyhound bus ticket in New York City stamped with Detroit as his destination. He got on the bus, settled down, read for a while, and then slept for most of the rest of the trip. When the bus stopped at other terminals, he would get out, use the restroom, and buy something to eat. Then he got back on the bus again.

When the bus pulled into the terminal of its final destination, the man collected his bag, walked through the terminal, and out onto the street. He asked someone which direction he should go to get to Woodward Avenue. Nobody seemed to know. He asked several more people how to get to Woodward Avenue, and each time he was met with blank stares.

Finally he got upset. "Come on," he shouted. "Woodward Avenue is Main Street here. I know Detroit!"

That's when they burst into laughter around him. "This isn't Detroit," they said. "This is Kansas City!"

He had gotten on the wrong bus.

Sometimes it's no big deal to get on the wrong bus or to take the wrong turn. You realize your mistake and then turn around and get back to where you were supposed to be. There are times, though, when taking a wrong turn can be much more serious.

It happened to me in the summer of 1977, when I was serving as a seminary intern at a church in Anchorage, Alaska. One of the families there had a rustic lake cabin, and they invited me to take all of the young people out there on a Saturday. The church was small, so all the young people could cram like sardines into one large station wagon.

Since I was not familiar with the lay of the land, Gwen served as navigator. Alaska is a huge state, but it has only six major highways. Just outside of Anchorage we had to turn right or left. Gwen said left, so that's the way we went.

An hour later I asked Gwen, for the tenth time, "Are you sure this is the right way? Do you recognize anything around here?"

When we finally stopped for help, we were about as far from where we wanted to be as we could get. We had to go back all the way to the fork in the road just outside of Anchorage before we could head in the right direction. When we finally arrived at the telephoneless cabin three hours late, our hosts were beside themselves with worry.

Catching the wrong bus or taking the wrong turn can be a problem. Jesus uses that as an illustration for religious decisions. "Enter through the narrow gate," he says. "For wide is the gate and broad is the road that leads to destruction, and many enter through it. But small is the gate and narrow the road that leads to life, and only a few find it."

What's the point?

GOOD INTENTIONS AREN'T ENOUGH

Jesus says that good intentions aren't enough in life. Remember his story of the Prodigal Son? The young man who left home didn't start out looking for a job feeding pigs. After he collected his inheritance, he set out to find happiness, freedom, friends, and adventure. But then he got on the wrong bus, and when they showed him where he had arrived, he knew just how foolish he had been.

I think of that, sometimes, when I am officiating at a marriage ceremony. What exciting times! Everyone smiles. Everybody is dressed up for a celebration. Everything is so beautiful, so radiant, so full of hope and promise.

I stand at the front of the church with the bride and groom, and in their eyes I see the best of intentions—theirs will be the perfect marriage. Theirs will be the strongest home. Theirs will be the deepest vows, the truest commitments, the richest promises, and the surest future.

Yet, within me, there is often this nagging uncertainty. Why, for so many who think they are headed for heaven, does the journey of marriage lead them to hell? I pray for every marriage, "Lord, let them get on the right bus." Good intentions aren't enough.

Hector Berlioz, the great composer, was living in Paris in 1830. He loved a young woman named Camille, and they were engaged to be married.

But then Hector was awarded the Prix de Roma, the Prize of Rome. He could study and compose and perform his music in Italy for a year or two, and all of his financial needs would be covered.

Camille agreed with him that this was an opportunity he needed to take advantage of. Off he went, with a kiss, and a promise that they would soon be married. His intentions never changed.

But life in Rome swallowed him up. And for Camille, life in Paris went on. Other suitors came to call. When Berlioz next heard from her, she was on her way to marry another. Hector, of course, caught the next coach to Paris. Only he got on the wrong one and ended up in Genoa. There he tried again. He booked passage to France once more, but his anxiety must have blinded him because he took the wrong coach again and ended up in Nice.

By this time Camille was married, and Hector quit his journey. That's what happens, sometimes, when you catch the wrong bus.

The world is full of good intentions. Nobody wants war. Everybody wants prosperity. There is a hope and a wish and a desire for love in every human heart. But read the morning newspaper or watch the evening news and another picture emerges. The best of intentions isn't enough to heal the racial scars in Los Angeles. The highest ambitions can't lift the slums of Calcutta out of hell. The purest desires won't, by themselves, chart a course to peace, prosperity, and democracy among the countries of the former Soviet Union.

Having an ideal, catching a vision, or knowing which city you want to go to doesn't get you there. That's the point of the saying, "The road to hell is paved with good intentions." That's what Jesus is speaking of in Matthew 7:13–14..

Do you think that those who sit in A. A. meetings dreamed in their younger years that they would find themselves there some day? Of course not. And when they come to that point, when they find themselves in a city they didn't intend to visit, when they know that they took the wrong bus somewhere, what do they do? Do they wish for another city and imagine it into being? The City of Sobriety? The Metropolis of Second Chances?

If you have ever gone to an A. A. meeting, you know it isn't so. The right bus comes, for them, only through hard work and mutual support and through watching every step of the journey. Late at night they call each other and say, "Get on the right bus. Stay on the wagon. Don't let your thirst take your feet where your heart knows it shouldn't go."

You see, actions have results. When the Watergate scandal broke years ago and President Nixon was forced to resign, Senator Sam Irvin of North Carolina said, "Do you know why this happened? Because they forgot that actions have consequences."

Rudyard Kipling once wrote a poem about that. He called it "The Gods of the Copybook Headings." It was all about those little lessons that we learned in elementary school. They were simple, but extremely important: water will make us wet, and fire will burn us; two and two are four, and pigs don't have wings; all that glitters is not necessarily gold, and the wages of sin is death.

Kipling said that if we forgot these fundamental rules of life, "the Gods of the Copybook Headings with terror and slaughter shall return." And so it is. Actions have consequences. Good intentions aren't enough. Do you want to go to Detroit? Then get on the right bus. Do you want to make your dreams come true? Then enter the journey of life through the right gate.

EVERY CHOICE IS A NEW GATE

Here's another implication to be drawn from Jesus' words in Matthew 7: Every choice is a new gate.

Think of it: hundreds, and maybe thousands, of people are scattered around Jesus as he speaks on the hillside. Each one of them is at a different stage of life. Some are grandmothers with market bags in hand, watching the children play in the meadow. Some are soldiers of fortune, marching to Palestine with the Roman legions because they want the taste of adventure and a chance to see the world. Some are poor folk, out scrounging the fields for tonight's meager fare. Some are educated teachers and some are reluctant students.

But to all of them, Jesus says the same thing: Find the right gate. Take the right bus. Make the right choices in life. And they can all act on Jesus' words because every choice in life is a new gate.

C. S. Lewis describes our lives so well in *Mere Christianity*. In the chapter on "Christian Behavior," he talks about people who think that Christianity is a kind of one-time bargain with God: You do this for me and I'll do that for you. We bargain our way into heaven based on a one-time negotiation.

Not so, says Lewis. That's not the way of the Bible. We aren't people who have managed to bargain our way into heaven. Rather, we are people who make choices. We all start out at a similar point when we enter this world as babies. But then we begin to choose. We choose this way instead of that; we choose these friends instead of those; we pick this career rather than the other.

Little by little, along the way, says Lewis, we begin to turn ourselves toward God or toward something else, something ultimately demonic. Each choice in life is a new gate. Which way will you go? Or, perhaps more accurately, who are you becoming?

Sometimes people ask about how they can know God's will. How do I know what God wants me to do in this situation? What does he want me to do with my life? Does he want me to go into medicine or accounting? How do I know?

When people come to me with such questions, I tell them the story about a fellow who was in love with two women, Susan and Sharon.

He wanted to get married, but he didn't know which one he should ask. How could he determine who the right woman was for him?

So he played Gideon's trick, as told in the book of Judges. Gideon thought God wanted him to do something, but he wasn't sure. So he prayed very passionately one night, "God, if you want me to do this, then I'm going to make it easy for you to tell me. I'm going to put out a big woolly fleece tonight. If you really want me to do this, let the dew cover the ground, but let the fleece be completely dry."

Wouldn't you know it? That's exactly what happened.

Of course, Gideon wasn't quite sure God had gotten the message straight, so the next night be prayed again: "Let's try this one more time, God. I'm not sure you heard me clearly last night. Why don't we turn it around tonight, just to be certain. If you want me to do this, make the ground all around dry tonight, with no dew. Then send all of that dew onto the fleece, soaking it so much that I'll know you heard me."

Once again God did his part, and finally Gideon went ahead with the task.

Now, this young man, whose heart was torn between Sharon and Susan, wanted to "pull a Gideon" on God. So he took out a quarter, looked toward heaven, and said to God, "Tell me whom I should marry. Heads it's Susan; tails it's Sharon."

He tossed the coin into the air and caught it on his arm. He peeked under his palm, and then looked back toward heaven and said, "How about two out of three?"

Isn't that a picture of us? He's not really looking for God's will; he's looking for God to confirm his own will. While that, in itself, is a wrong attitude, there is another problem in the whole scenario. God's will is rarely so small that it is merely this choice against that choice. God's will is a way of life, a series of choices, a decision that you keep on making. The two gates are always there in front of us, and it's not just a matter of picking up apples instead of oranges in the produce department. Rather, it's always a question of values, of motives, of desires. It's a matter of seeing the goal of our lives in our minds, and then getting on the right bus over and over and over again.

Says Lewis, "Every time you make a choice you are turning the central part of you, the part of you that chooses, into something a little different than it was before." He says that when you look at your life as a whole, with all of those innumerable choices you make from day to day, "all your life long you are slowly turning either into a heavenly creature or into a hellish creature."

It's not just Sharon or Susan. It's your life, your very soul. If you want love, then you can't have control.

If you're looking for peace, then don't try coercion. If sex means something to you, then don't think that pornography will get you there. It's the wrong bus. Do you want to find friends and conversation? Then you can't choose gossip. Those buses run on different schedules. Are you looking for God? Then get on the right bus again and again, at every stop along the road of your life.

Horace Bushnell, lecturing at Yale University long ago, told of his crisis of faith. He asked, was there really a God? Could he talk about a faith he didn't feel? How could he know the right way to go in his life?

He stopped one day and looked toward the destination he hoped to find. Then he thought to himself, "This I know, that truth is better than a lie; that love is better than hate; that courage is better than cowardice." With that in view, he began to make choices in life that would lead to those ends. He decided again and again to get on the right buses for those destinations.

Shortly before he died in 1876, Bushnell said to a friend, "I know Jesus Christ better than I know any man at Hartford." That faith didn't come by waltzing softly through life or by drifting along with the currents or by letting the winds blow him this way and that. It came for him each time he stood again at the gates, each time he had to make a choice in his life, each time he got on a bus, and he took it to the place where it was headed. The choices of his life brought him round again and again to God.

EARLIER DECISIONS INFLUENCE LATER DECISIONS

That brings us to a third reflection: earlier decisions influence later decisions.

Robert Frost summarizes it well in his famous poem "The Road Not Taken." He writes of finding himself in a forest of trees on a glorious autumn afternoon. He's walking down a path, and there's a fork in the way. Which direction should he go? When he makes his choice and picks his direction, he says to himself:

> I shall be telling this with a sigh
> Somewhere ages and ages hence:
> Two roads diverged in a wood, and I—
> I took the one less traveled by,
> And that has made all the difference.

That's the way it is in life. Years ago you chose to settle in this town and your decision has had lasting effects. You chose your course of education. Think of what you could have been if you had gone into engineering instead of medicine. But think also of who you have become because of the decision you made way back then.

You chose your friends, and they have made you into something too. You chose your spouse, you chose your house, you chose your church. And see what you have become because of it all.

Earlier decisions influence later decisions. Because you chose the career you did, you have touched people in a new way. Because you chose your friends well, you have become more friendly, more loving, more trusting. Think of what you would be like today if you had stayed in that crowd you used to run with.

And because you chose your church, you have grown in Christ. You have learned of the grace of God, of the strength of his holiness, of the joy of service and fellowship and commitment.

Your earlier decisions have influenced you along the way.

George Mueller was one of the finest persons who ever walked this earth. In the last century he set up orphanages around the world to care for the little ones who had no one else to look after them. He provided for the poor. He preached the love of Jesus, and he lived it every day.

Someone once called him a success. He said no, he wasn't a success, only a servant, a servant of his master who had loved him to life.

Well, said the reporter, how did you manage to do all you've done during the course of your life?

"I don't really know," said George Mueller. "As I look back on my life, I see that I was constantly brought to a crossroads which demanded a choice of which way I should go." He said that once he had started to follow in the steps of Jesus, all the rest of the decisions that came after seemed easier. He caught the right bus. When he had done that the first time it became the start of a habit. The second time he knew which bus to take, and by the third and the fourth and the fifth choices, the way was much more clear. Earlier decisions made his later decisions easier.

Robert Maynard once told how he became a writer. The journey began when he was a young boy walking to school one morning. He came to a fresh patch of concrete in the sidewalk. Somebody had just finished troweling it smooth, and it was just waiting for him.

He bent over to write his name in the cement, when suddenly there was a hulking shadow engulfing him. Looking up in terror, he saw the biggest construction mason he had ever seen in his life. The guy was holding a garbage can lid, ready to smash the first little kid who dared mess up his new sidewalk.

Maynard says he tried to run, but the guy caught him around the waist and shouted, "What do you think you're doing? Why are you trying to spoil my work?"

Maynard remembers babbling something about only wanting to write his name there for everyone to see.

The man's eyes softened. He set young Maynard on the ground and said, "Look at me, son. What do you want to be when you grow up?"

Maynard squeaked out, "A writer, I think."

The man sat there with him for a moment, and then pointed to the school across the street. He said, "If you want to write your name where it really matters, then go to that school and learn what it takes and become a real writer. And then, someday, write your name on the cover of a book, and let the whole world see it."

That, says Robert Maynard, was the day he became a writer. The first decision was made that day, and every choice he's had to make along the way has been easier because someone helped him to know who he really was. Someone showed him early on how to make a good choice —took his hand at a critical moment and led him to the right bus.

That's why we need to be concerned about the younger members of our community and the education they receive. The younger we are when we find the right bus in life, the easier it is to work our way through other crowded bus stations later on in our lives. Earlier decisions influence later decisions, and no young child makes a right or wrong decision by himself or herself. He or she is led to that decision by the hand of some bigger person who says, "This is what your life is all about. If you want to find out what that means, this is the bus you're going to have to take."

Do you remember the ancient Greek legend of the Minotaur? The Minotaur was a terrible monster that lived deep underground in a labyrinth of caves and passages. Every year the Minotaur devoured young children.

Someone had to put a stop to it, so young Theseus volunteered. He went down into the realms of darkness, took his sword, braved the beast, and slew it dead. But how would he get out of the labyrinth? How would he take the right turns and pass through the right gates in this maze? Everyone who saw him enter the deadly chasm was sure that he would never return to the surface, even though the Minotaur had stopped its fierce bellowing.

There was one person, however, who never stopped hoping. She loved Theseus, and knew that he would return. She knew it because she had handed him a ball of string before he left on his mission. And there, in the land where he was loved, in the place where he belonged, he tied one end of that string.

After he destroyed the cruel beast in the maze, all he had to do was follow the string of his love. It opened the right doors and took him on the right paths. It marked the right gates and led him to the place he knew he had to reach. The string of his love helped him catch the right bus.

That's the gospel for us. All our education, all our training, and all our decision-making is, in some way, following the string that was handed to us by others.

One time, long ago, when the labyrinth of life around us was roaring with the rough meanness of the Minotaur, a young man came into our caves and our dark passages. He found the beast and slew it. Then he did one more thing. He handed us a golden string: the way out, the way of life, the ticket on the right bus.

Listen to the words of William Blake. They are really the words of Jesus. He says to us:

I give you the end of a golden string;
Only wind it into a ball,
It will lead you in at Heaven's gate,
Built in Jerusalem's wall.

Have you found that string? Are you on the right bus in life? And are you bringing the little ones along by the hand?

"Watch out for false prophets. They come to you in sheep's clothing, but inwardly they are ferocious wolves. By their fruit you will recognize them. Do people pick grapes from thornbushes, or figs from thistles? Likewise every good tree bears good fruit, but a bad tree bears bad fruit. A good tree cannot bear bad fruit, and a bad tree cannot bear good fruit. Every tree that does not bear good fruit is cut down and thrown into the fire. Thus, by their fruit you will recognize them.

"Not everyone who says to me, 'Lord, Lord,' will enter the kingdom of heaven, but only he who does the will of my Father who is in heaven. Many will say to me on that day, 'Lord, Lord, did we not prophesy in your name, and in your name drive out demons and perform many miracles?' Then I will tell them plainly, 'I never knew you. Away from me, you evildoers!'

"Therefore everyone who hears these words of mine and puts them into practice is like a wise man who built his house on the rock. The rain came down, the streams rose, and the winds blew and beat against that house; yet it did not fall, because it had its foundation on the rock. But everyone who hears these words of mine and does not put them into practice is like a foolish man who built his house on sand. The rain came down, the streams rose, and the winds blew and beat against that house, and it fell with a great crash."

When Jesus had finished saying these things, the crowds were amazed at his teaching, because he taught as one who had authority, and not as their teachers of the law.

—Matthew 7:15–29

15
DEFINING YOUR DESTINY

Setting Our Sights by the Morning Star

SOME YEARS AGO, *Newsweek* magazine reported a fortune tellers' convention in Dublin, Ireland. Palm readers, crystal ball gazers, and astrologers from all over the world gathered for a week to compare notes, learn techniques, and make new predictions. While they were all together in one of the convention meetings, a thief broke into the hotel rooms and stole all the crystal balls and tarot cards.

When the police investigated the crime, they asked the fortune tellers, "Didn't you know this was going to happen? Why weren't you able to predict it?"

The future is not always as easy to see as we might hope. Eighteenth-century shoemaker John Partridge thought he would try his hand at predicting. He published a journal called the *Partridge Almanac.* Partridge was particularly proud of his weather forecasting ability and featured it prominently in each issue.

Traveling through the English countryside, Partridge stayed overnight at an inn. The next morning, when he prepared to leave, a stable hand cautioned him against traveling that day. "It's going to rain a good one," he said.

Partridge glanced up at the early morning sky. It looked fine to him, so he set out. Before long a fierce thunderstorm forced him to turn back and seek shelter at the previous night's inn. The stable hand was there, grinning. "I told you so!"

Partridge was annoyed. "How did you know it was going to rain like that today?"

"Well," said the fellow, "we have one of those *Partridge Almanac*s here . . ."

John Partridge smiled.

The stable hand finished, ". . . and that fellow is such a liar. Whenever he predicts a good day we know for sure that it's going to rain!"

Most of us would like to know something about the future. In fact, it would be nice to be able to predict a few things about it. There is a sense in which Jesus concludes the Sermon on the Mount with the hint that that is possible.

YOU CHOOSE YOUR FUTURE

It is an incredible thought, but Jesus says that each of us chooses our own future.

That seems impossible, since so much of life appears to be thrown at us. "You have to take what comes to you," we tell each other. "Roll with the punches. *Que sera, sera*. What will be will be."

And so it is with many things. We don't choose to be born. We don't bargain for our inherited looks. Researchers say that 60 percent of all men and 90 percent of all women would like to change their appearance if they could. In little ways we can, but most of us live with the genetic mix tossed our way at conception.

It's that way in other aspects of our lives as well. In a powerful scene from Morris West's novel *The Clowns of God,* a father and daughter are having an argument. She tells him that she's going to Paris to live with her boyfriend. He won't let her. Why would she want to do something like that, he asks. She tells him that she is afraid.

"Afraid of what?"

"I'm afraid of getting married and having children and trying to make a home," she says, "while the whole world could tumble round our ears in a day. You older ones don't understand. You've survived a war. You've built things. You've raised families. But look at the world you've left to us. You've given us everything except tomorrow."

Everything except tomorrow. Yet tomorrow is the one thing that we need most. One newspaper carried this ad in its Classified section: "Hope chest—Brand new. Half price. Long story." We've had so many long stories in our lives, and so many broken promises, and so many shattered dreams. Sometimes we're ready to give up. No more promises. No more commitments.

Greek novelist Nikos Kazantzakis had these words chiseled onto his tombstone when he died: "I hope for nothing. I fear nothing. I am free."

But Jesus says in this passage, that's not freedom. That's not really what you want, is it?—no hope, no future, only a cold grave and a stone memorial. Then he offers us something better. Choose the doorway to your tomorrow, he says. Determine your own destiny.

How do we do that?

KNOW WHERE YOU WANT TO GO

It begins when we know where we want to go. What do you want out of life? Where do you hope to be ten or twenty years from now? Why do you hope to be there?

During World War II, the English government knew that Hitler was planning to invade the British Isles. They encouraged the people to prepare as best they could. They bolstered defenses on the southeast corner. They stationed reserve guards on constant watch. They developed early warning systems and evacuation routes for the people near the coast.

Then they did one more thing. The government passed a law requiring every community to take down all road signs and every other sign that named any town or village. They knew the Germans had maps of England, but if the invaders couldn't locate themselves on those maps, they would be slowed in their progress toward London. Without points of reference, the troops would wander aimlessly.

That's also the way it is in our lives. If we have no plans or hopes or goals, we find ourselves on the broad way that Jesus talks about in

Matthew 7:13. We go with the flow. We follow the crowd. We get on the treadmill with everyone else and are worn down by the same daily grind. "If you don't know where you are going," says the Koran, "any old road will get you there."

To live in a different way requires some goals that pull us toward the narrow path that leads to the Kingdom of God. Goals don't have to be big or outlandish or extravagant. They do, however, have to be important. In the preface to his magnificent novel *Moby Dick*, Herman Melville says, "To write a mighty book you must have a mighty theme."

It is similarly so on the pages of life. How do you see the world? Do you see it like God sees it? Do you know what he is planning with it? Do you understand his purposes for the world, and the meaning he gives to human existence? Have you found the road that leads to Life?

When the BBC wanted to do a program on the work of Mother Teresa in Calcutta, she at first refused. She didn't want publicity and didn't think it would be worth their while or her time. She certainly did not want to be famous.

Finally Malcolm Muggeridge talked her into it. He helped her to see that others needed her vision, her sense of purpose, her understanding of what God means for life. When he explained it to her like that, she became excited. "Yes," she said. "Malcolm, let's do it. Let's do something beautiful for God!"

That became the title of the program: "Something Beautiful for God."

If that is what a person wants in life, she's on the right road.

It reminds me of the story of Caleb in the Old Testament. Joshua is dividing Palestine for the tribes of Israel to settle. Caleb, at age eighty-five, is the oldest man in the community. He goes to Joshua and says something like, "Don't give me any of that seacoast, or any of those river valleys where the fishing is good and the farming is easy. Give me the hill country of Hebron. I want something I can wrestle with, something that will challenge me and keep me busy. Give me something I can make beautiful for God."

He's eighty-five years old, and that's the goal of his life. He knows which road he is on.

KEEP MAKING CHOICES

It isn't enough, however, to know where you want to go in life. It is just as important to keep making choices that put your feet on that path. Jesus says that many people say, "Lord, Lord!" but their talk is cheap, and their walk doesn't make it into the kingdom.

A woman once came running up to Arthur Rubinstein after he finished another spectacular concert. "Oh, Mr. Rubinstein!" she said, "I've always wanted to play the piano! I'd give anything if I could play like you did this evening!"

"No, you wouldn't," he replied. "I know what I've had to give up to be able to play like this, and if that's what you really wanted, you would have done the same."

It's true. He knew his goal. He knew where he wanted to be in life, and then he kept making the necessary choices. He practiced his scales. He put in his hours at the keyboard. He did what he had to do.

That's what Jesus talks about in verses 15–23. We all want to take a shortcut, he says. We're all looking for a quick fix, a get-rich-quick scheme, a way to double our income and cut our work in half. There are all kinds of voices out there telling us how to do it. Don't listen to them, says Jesus. They'll only bring you ruin in the end.

Of course, he should know. Over and over during his life on earth, people kept telling him how to get to his goal without making the necessary choices. "Let me make you a king," said the devil. "You know you've got it coming to you anyway."

Or there was Peter, his friend, saying, "Let me fight your battles for you, Lord! I've got a sharp sword, and it's ready for action."

Or listen to Mary Magdalene: "Stay with me, Jesus. I'll take care of you."

And he knows he deserves to be king. He knows how nice it would be to have others fight his battles. He knows what comfort Mary can give him. But he has a goal, and his goal requires choices only he can make. That is his destiny. So it is with us.

There is a powerful scene in Shakespeare's drama *The Merchant of Venice*. Portia is a beautiful, wealthy woman. Men come from all over the world begging to marry her. They have a goal in mind, but if they want to win her hand, they must first make a choice.

Portia knows that talk is often cheap, so she has had three large caskets created, and she uses them in a test of values. Whoever would win her hand must choose the casket that contains her portrait.

Each casket is very different from the others. One is made of silver, with an inscription that reads, "Who chooseth me shall get as much as he deserves." Those who are attracted to the shine of that fair vessel open it only to find the head of a fool. That, according to Portia, is what seekers of treasure deserve.

The second casket is even more spectacular than the first. It is gilded, and studded with baubles and gems. The inscription on this glittering icon reads, "Who chooseth me shall get what many men desire." The suitors who nod for this prize open it to receive a dry and lifeless skull. Riches are dead. They have no life in them.

Of course, there is the third casket, but it is rather ugly. It is only made of lead, and fashioned by a rather crude artisan. The message carved on the front is this: "Who chooseth me must give all and hazard all he hath." It is, however, the one which contains Portia's portrait.

This is the way it is on the narrow path to the Kingdom of God. If you own this goal, then this goal must own you. There are no shortcuts. There are no detours or safety measures. That is why Jesus pictures the gate as straight and the way narrow—no one can take along any treasures or safety gear. Choosing this way is a hazard. It's all or nothing.

This is how we begin to determine our destiny. It is not so much a matter of achieving our own ends as it is that of choosing to risk everything for the sake of finding something that matters. When we think about who we are today, there are a number of things that make each of us unique. There are, of course, our physical characteristics. Each of us is built a little differently than the next. That's what makes a community so interesting. It takes all kinds.

But our identities are much more than our appearances. There is a self that is much deeper, much more internal. It has to do with the way we think, with the feelings that pump through us, with the facts we know, and the desires that drive us. These things, when all is said and done, are mostly the result of the choices we have made along the way in life.

Marriage, for instance, doesn't happen overnight. You chose to get acquainted with someone. You chose to keep seeing him. You chose to commit yourself. You chose to plan a wedding. And every day you choose again to stay together.

The same is true of a career. You chose to stay in high school, even when your buddies dropped out. You chose to keep your grades up. You chose to apply to a variety of colleges. You chose courses that interested you. You chose a major. You put the money down each year. When it came time to graduate, you were at a different place in life than when you entered college, and the path you owned had begun to own you.

We choose our houses. We choose our clothes, our friends, our work and play. Even when a tragedy comes our way, something unplanned and unexpected, like a death or an illness or a divorce, we still choose how we deal with it. We choose to turn it into something we can live with. And in those choices we find ourselves.

"The greatest thing in the world," said Oliver Wendell Holmes, "is not so much where we stand, as in what direction we are moving." In that sense we define our destiny and predict our futures. Our life choices become the key to knowing who we are and what we are becoming.

YOUR FUTURE CHOOSES YOU

But the gospel is found in one more word. Jesus tells it in the story of the two builders, one foolish, one wise. Palestine is not a friendly place for construction. Much of the landscape is uneven with rocks and boulders. It takes a lot of effort to lay a straight foundation on the sloping and convoluted surfaces, where no spade will dig.

There are, of course, the low spots in the waddies between the hills. Here the sands have trickled to form a flat and even bed. It is easy to begin construction, and the walls of the rocky waddies seem to stand as security fences all around. To the human eye the builder who struggles to erect a house on the rocky slopes seems foolish—his efforts exceed the return. Meanwhile, the builder on the sands of the waddies seems to have chosen wisely. Construction speeds ahead, and he is living in his mansion before the other house even has a roof.

That's the human view. But the wise becomes foolish when the spring rains in the mountains run off in a crazed tumult through the slits in the rocks and erase all memory of human construction on the sands. And the foolish becomes wise when the house on the rocks above becomes a safe haven from the restless tide below.

The message is clear. When you have determined your own destiny, your destiny begins to determine you. When you choose a future wisely or foolishly, your future begins to confirm your choice, for good or ill.

And somehow, in the great grace of God, when we find ourselves on the road to his house, to his glory, to his love, he is the one who makes sure that we go all the way. In the end it is his strength and power that takes us by the hand and leads us along the path to the kingdom. The old hymn "I Sought the Lord" says it so well:

> I sought the Lord and afterward I knew:
> He moved my soul to seek him seeking me!
> 'Twas not so much that I on Thee took hold,
> As Thou, dear Lord, on me, on me!
>
> I find, I walk, I love; but O the whole
> Of love is but my answer, Lord, to Thee!
> For Thou wert long beforehand with my soul;
> Always, always, Thou lovedst me!

Donna Hoffman, a young Christian mother who battled cancer for a number of years, wrote this poem in her journal. She was in the hospital at the time, and the cancer seemed so strong. She calls her poem "Journey":

> My soul runs
> arms outstretched down the corridor to you.
>
> Ah, my feet may stumble
> but how my heart can stride!

That's the testimony of those who know their futures. That's the strength of those who have determined their destinies. That's the heart of those who know their goals, and who make their daily choices. It is God's grace that sustains them, even when their feet stumble and even when the journey seems too long. "How my heart can stride," they say. "For the goal of my life, the glory of my God, has taken hold of me."

Generations ago young William Borden went to Yale University. He was the wealthy son of a powerful family. He could choose to do anything with his life. After he graduated, he chose to become a missionary of the gospel of Jesus Christ. His friends thought he was crazy. "Why throw away your life like that?" they asked.

But Borden knew his future. He determined his destiny. He made his choices, and his goals laid hold of him. He set out on a long journey to China. In those days it took months. By the time he got to Egypt some disease ravaged his body. He was placed in a hospital. Soon it became obvious that he would never recover. William Borden would die a foreigner in Egypt. He never reached his goal, and he never went back home.

He could have thought, "What a waste. I should have listened to my family. I should have stayed in America. Why did God do this to me?"

Those, however, were not his dying thoughts. His last conscious act was to write a little note. Seven words that were spoken at his funeral. Seven words that summarized his life, his goals, his choices, and his identity: "No reserve, no retreat, and no regrets!"

Can you say that? "No reserve, no retreat, and no regrets!"

Does that describe who you are? Can you see your future? Have you determined your destiny? Then I send you on your way with the words of an old Irish blessing:

> May the road rise to meet you.
> May the wind be always at your back.
> May the sun shine warm on your face,
> and the rain fall softly on your fields;
> And until we meet again,
> may God hold you in the palm of his hand!

ABOUT THE AUTHOR

WAYNE BROUWER IS the husband of Brenda (*nee:* Karsten), and they are parents of three daughters, Kristyn, Kimberly, and Kaitlyn. Wayne has pastored congregations in Alberta and Ontario, Canada, and has served as a missionary teacher in Nigeria. He has written more than five hundred articles that have appeared in journals such as *Leadership, Christianity Today, Preaching,* and *Vital Ministry,* and has authored a number of books including *Walking on Water, With New and Open Eyes,* and *Hear Me, O God*. He is Senior Pastor of Harderwyk Christian Reformed Church in Holland, Michigan. He holds degrees from Dordt College (B.A.), Calvin Theological Seminary (M.Div., Th.M.), and McMaster University (M.A., Ph.D.).